Common Bonds and Cultural Traditions of the People of the US and Japan

Kenneth J. M. MacLean and Nobuhiro Suzuki

Common Bonds and Cultural Traditions of the people of the US and Japan.

ISBN: 978-1-61599-863-0

Cover photo credit: Library of Congress, Prints & Photographs Division, photograph by Harris & Ewing, [reproduction number, e.g., LC-USZ62-123456]. Original photo cropped by the author. There are no known copyright restrictions on this photograph.

Contents

Introduction

It is getting easier to obtain information from different countries because of globalization and advances in technology. Nevertheless, I am not sure if we are better able to understand the cultures and customs of other countries. I feel that conflicts between people and countries are increasing rather than decreasing. This situation may be due to a lack of mutual understanding.

Each of us should think about how different countries with different cultural backgrounds can coexist on the earth. In this book, Ken and I will share a layman's view of the world. I hope that this book will help you realize that you don't have to be an expert to think about the world.

— *Nobuhiro Suzuki, March 2023*

In this book Nobuhiro and I attempt to identify cultural and historical differences and similarities between Japan and the United States, with the aim of increasing understanding between the two countries and their people. Most Americans know little about Japanese culture or history, and most Japanese only know America through entertainment programs, movies, and corporate media, which does not reflect the views of a significant proportion of Americans.

We began this effort in 2020 during the Pandemic. The political and cultural changes that have resulted have, certainly in the US, created a far more polarized society. Learning about another culture can be beneficial to Americans, who use social media mostly to scream and yell at each other!

Neither Nobu or I are historians. We have approached this effort strictly from a layman's point of view. We wanted to share a layman's view of the world, not an "expert" one. I come from a working class family from Detroit. Nobu is a botanist and professor at a Japanese university, so we see things from different perspectives.

In Chapter 1 we present a brief history of the two countries, as an introduction to the rest of the book.

In Chapter 2 we outline the culture of each country by describing the life of a "typical" citizen in Japan and in the US.

Chapter 3 speaks to the relationship between the US and Japan.

In Chapter 4 we address the effects of the 2020 election in the US, which not only created great conflict in the United States, but has led to a fracturing of the previous world order that was previously dominated by the US. We picked up news sources in Japan and in the US before and after the election, and commented on them.

Chapter 5 discusses the effects of the 2020 pandemic on the people of the US and Japan.

Chapter 6, titled "A New World Order," discusses the conflict between the two major political and economic systems that are competing for supremacy on the world stage.

Finally, Chapter 7 briefly outlines what a true world community would look like.

We both hope you enjoy this modest effort.

— *Kenneth MacLean, March 2023*

Map of Japan from japanmap360.com

— 1 —

A Brief Cultural History of the US and Japan

A Brief History of Japan – by Nobuhiro Suzuki

Introduction

Japanese culture has been developed based on its long history. Japan's agricultural, island-based history strongly affects the creation of Japanese characteristics and harmonious personal relations. Here, we will not attempt to describe the entirety of Japanese history. However, history and culture that might influence characteristics of Japan will be introduced.

Foundation

First-century Japan was a collection of over 100 small, independent countries located at various parts of the island. From this time on, the number of countries gradually decreased because of the consolidation and unifications between these countries. By the fourth century, one relatively large country in the Kansai area (currently around Osaka and Kyoto) had grown to particular prominence. The family which ruled this country in the final stages of its consolidation became the imperial family (currently called the "Tennou" family). In Japan, the "***Emperor's birthday***" is still a holiday (in Japanese, "Tennou Tanjou-bi," Tanjou-bi means birthday).

The foundation of Japan was a gradual process that continued over many years. It is therefore impossible to set any particular year and date as that on which the nation came into existence. In the two ancient chronicles written in the eighth century, it is recorded that the Emperor Jinmu began his reign in the year 660 BC and the date given for his ascension, February 11, is currently set as "***National Foundation Day.***"

Religion

The principal religions in Japan are Shinto and Buddhism. Interestingly, few Japanese are deeply devoted to a specific religion, and indeed, many profess to have no interest in religion.

In a country with the beauty of nature and a moderate four-season climate, Japanese have for many generations led an easygoing existence free from the threat of natural disasters and the invasion of enemies. (However, the situation is changing and Japan has recently suffered from natural disasters such as earthquakes and flooding.) Perhaps because of this, Japanese have not developed any deep religious yearning. In addition, Shintoism, the religion of Japan from time untold, is polytheistic. Because of this the Japanese people have traditionally been tolerant of all religious sects.

Interestingly, the birth and marriage ceremonies of most Japanese are held with a Shinto or Christianity style, while funerals are Buddhist style. The same persons will pay their respects to a Shinto shrine at the beginning of the year, visit a Buddhist temple during the Festival of the Souls in summer called "Obon," and celebrate Christmas at the end of the year. The number of followers are: Shinto, 108 million; Buddhism, 94 million; and Christianity, 2.2 million. The sum of these figures is nearly twice the population of Japan, a situation without parallel in other countries. The Japanese constitution guarantees religious freedom, and this guarantee is strictly maintained. There is no state religion, and no connection between national and religious functions.

History

Until 10,000–20,000 years ago, Japan was still connected to the Asian continent by land. As a result of movement of the earth's crust and elevation in sea level, Japan was completely separated from other regions of Asia. As an island country, Japan has not been susceptible to invasion but, being relatively close to the other Asian countries, it has had relatively easy access to advanced foreign cultures. It might be asked why Japan possesses a common culture with other countries while simultaneously maintaining a highly specific "Japanese" culture. The history of Japan is briefly summarized below.

Kofun Period

Around the 1st century BC, there were about 100 small countries that interacted independently with China and incorporated its culture and technology. In the 2nd century, conflicts between these countries escalated until a woman named "Himiko" became the king of the Allied Powers, settling the fighting and creating the Allied nation "Yamatai."

In the 3rd century, powerful people built large tombs called *Kofun* to display their power. More than 200 pieces were made all over the country, which is also the origin of the name of the Kofun Period.

In the 4th century, the Yamato administration was established, which was a coalition nation headed by Okimi and unified the small nations in each region. However, when the country grew, the Great King alone could not manage everything. The governance system consisted of various positions such as diplomacy, armament, accounting, and land management, but it was still a confederation where small countries were placed under the control of the Yamato administration, and each country organized its own region.

Asuka Period

This is the era of the power struggle between the Soga clan, in charge of finance, and the Mononobe clan, in charge of the military, during the Yamato administration. In the Asuka period, the Soga and Mononobe clans constantly fought each other, with the Soga clan advocating for the acceptance of Buddhism, while the Mononobe opposed it. The conflict resulted in the Soga clan destroying the Mononobe clan and the assassination of Emperor Sushun in 592 by Soga no Umako.

Prince Shotoku became the supporter of Empress Suiko. Prince Shotoku adopted the ideas of Confucianism and Buddhism and laid the foundation for the imperial court system by creating a constitution called the "Seventeen-Article Constitution." This may be the first constitution in Japan. In addition, a new system of recruitment of officials, called the "12 Level Cap and Rank System" was established, in which the rank and promotion of officials were determined based on skills and individual achievement.

Conflict inside Japan

In Japan, many countries were always fighting for political power and land. Samurai played active roles during this period.

The lord of a small land fought with the lord of the neighboring land and expanded his power, and when he continued to win repeatedly, he became the lord of a nation. Then, in order to get another country, he started a battle by attacking the neighboring country. Such conflicts were repeated all over Japan.

Nara Period

This is the era when the capital was Heijo-kyo in Nara, for 84 years from 710 to 794. In this period, the development of the country and the improvement of the governance system were promoted. Combined with communication with the Tang and Korea, and the rise of Buddhism, Japanese culture and arts flourished.

Heian Period

The Heian Period refers to the approximately 390 years from when the Emperor moved the capital to Heian-kyo (Kyoto, present-day Kyoto City, Kyoto Prefecture) in 794, until the establishment of the Kamakura Shogunate. It is called the Heian Period because it was almost the only center of politics until the shogunate was established. It is usually placed at the end of ancient times, but it is also possible to place it in the embryonic period of the Middle Ages. It is understood as a transitional period from ancient times to the Middle Ages.

From the first half to the middle of the Heian period, the Fujiwara clan rose to power in the capital. During the Heian period, the Fujiwara clan gained power in the capital by marrying their daughters to emperor princesses and making their children the next emperor.

During the Heian period, samurai emerged in rural areas due to neglect by the aristocrats in the capital, who were preoccupied with their own power struggles. With no one to control criminal activity, people took matters into their own hands and said, "It can't be helped, we have no choice but to protect ourselves." This led to the emergence of the samurai.

As samurai gained power, politics changed. Emperor Gosanjo, who had a weak relationship with the Fujiwara clan, promoted political reforms, and Emperor Shirakawa, who followed him, wielded political power. As a result of two civil wars over politics, the Hogen Rebellion and Heiji Rebellion broke out in Kyoto, with involvement from the Minamoto and Taira clans. Taira no Kiyomori emerged victorious in the Heiji War, expanded his power, and began influencing politics.

Taira no Kiyomori helped the retired Emperor Goshirakawa with his cloistered government, and he himself wielded power as Dajodaijin. In addition, he actively embarked on trade with the Song dynasty in China and established a samurai government. The Taira clan controlled politics as they wished, but dissatisfaction with the aristocrats, temples, and local samurai increased. Minamoto no Yoritomo, who controlled Kamakura, sent his younger brother Minamoto no Yoshitsune and others to Dannoura in Yamaguchi Prefecture to destroy the Taira clan.

Kamakura Period

Minamoto no Yoritomo took control of politics from the Taira clan and established his base in Kamakura. He was appointed by Emperor Gotoba to the position that controlled politics. However, after Yoritomo's death and the assassination of the second and third shoguns, the Minamoto clan was defeated. A dispute broke out among the Samurai, and Hojo Tokimasa, who had gathered together the powerful Samurai, seized power. The Hojo clan suppressed the power of the shogun and assumed the position of regent, and moved politics. The Kamakura shogunate, established in 1192, continued for over 200 years under the reign of the

Hojo clan. However, Emperor Godaigo's army overthrew the shogunate in 1333, destroying it in just one year.

Muromachi Period

When the Kamakura shogunate collapsed, a new emperor-centered government began under Emperor Godaigo. However, the samurai were opposed to this.

Ashikaga Takauji defected and raised an army, and the new government collapsed in about two years. After the Onin War, which started in Kyoto in 1467, the power of the Muromachi shogunate finally weakened, and the samurais, called Sengoku daimyo, increased their power in rural areas.

The Warring States period begins, and war breaks out in various places. Nobunaga Oda and Hideyoshi Toyotomi put an end to these wars. Oda Nobunaga practically destroyed the Muromachi Shogunate in 1573, and Japan entered the Azuchi-Momoyama period.

Azuchi Momoyama period

After the fall of the Muromachi shogunate, Oda Nobunaga gradually strengthened his power. However, Nobunaga was attacked and destroyed in a rebellion by his subordinate, Mitsuhide Akechi. This is the "Honnoji Incident" of 1582.

After defeating Nobunaga, Akechi Mitsuhide was thought to be the replacement for Nobunaga. Hideyoshi Toyotomi challenged Akechi Mitsuhide as an enemy of Nobunaga, and destroyed Akechi Mitsuhide. Then, Hideyoshi Toyotomi took over Japan.

When Hideyoshi Toyotomi died, Tokugawa Ieyasu began to move to become the next ruler of Japan. But Mitsunari Ishida, who had continued to loyally support the Toyotomi family, stood up and challenged in battle to prevent Ieyasu from conquering Japan. This is called the Battle of Sekigahara, the big and important battle in 1600. Ieyasu Tokugawa led the Eastern Army to victory in this battle. He defeated the Western Army led by Mitsunari Ishida at Sekigahara. Tokugawa started to accumulate political power in Japan, and the Edo period began.

Edo Period

After the end of the era of conflicts, the Edo period started. The Edo period began in 1603 after Ieyasu Tokugawa became the general who was the highest military authority. Tokugawa established a government called "Shogun" in Edo (present-day Tokyo). It lasted about 260 years until it collapsed in 1868.

The Feudal system in Japan began during the Kamakura Period. After that the system was improved and developed, and then established during Edo period.

The Feudal system is a social and political system in which the princes under the monarch occupy the land and govern the people on the land.

I feel that this hierarchical relationship still remains strong in Japanese society. For example, at school, there is a hierarchical relationship between seniors and juniors. And even if they start working in society, there is still a strong tendency that makes it difficult for subordinates to go against what their boss says. Perhaps this tendency in Japan was established during this era.

Era of isolation (Sakoku)

During the Edo period in the 17th century, Japan closed all relations with foreign countries and entered a period of isolation known as "Sakoku."

During this period, manufacturing and commerce became increasingly important, and the merchants were able to develop economic power. As a result, the power of warriors as the ruling classes began to decline.

A long, peaceful period during the 18th and 19th centuries also affected the power of warriors.

In addition, rapid cultural and educational advances were achieved during this historical period. It is likely that such changes provided the foundation for the modern Japanese nation.

Resumption of overseas trade (Kaikoku)

In 1842, the great power of Asia, Qing (China), lost the war with Britain, who opened the country. The Shogunate, which had a sense of crisis about this, eased Japan's seclusion policy.

In 1853, Matthew Calbraith Perry from the USA led four warships and urged the Shogunate to open the country against the backdrop of his mighty military power. At this time, the Shogunate negotiated well and managed to postpone Perry's demands for a year. However, in 1854, Perry again led seven warships. Fearing the mighty military power, the shogunate succumbed to Perry's pressure and ended Japan's seclusion system.

In 1858, Townsend Harris from the USA arrived in Japan. The shogunate was forced to sign unfavorable treaties, such as not being able to freely impose tariffs and not being able to judge foreigners in Japan even for problems that arose while they were in Japan. Signing a disadvantageous treaty with the United States put pressure on the Netherlands, Russia, Great Britain, and France as well, and eventually the shogunate signed an unequal treaty with those countries.

Meiji Period

The Meiji era was a turning point in history. The Meiji government, which led Japan after the Edo Shogunate, promoted the modernization of the country through "civilization" that actively adopted the advanced systems and culture of the West.

The government was managed by laws such as the Constitution of the Empire of Japan, and the tax system was reviewed. Education, postal systems, and railroads were born. Many of the foundations of what shapes Japan's society today were laid down in this era.

Behind the modernization was the idea of "de-Asia entry": to leave Asia and be on a par with Western countries.

Taisho Period

World War I had a significant impact on Japan's economy, expanding its interests as it received many military orders from the Allies. This led to a rise in the number of wealthy people, but also a widening gap between the rich and poor, and a subsequent economic downturn after the war.

In 1920, the League of Nations was formed as the world's first international peace organization. From 1920 to 1939, 63 nations, including Japan, became member states. In this way, the momentum for international cooperation increased both in Japan and around the world.

In Japan, the movement toward democracy and liberalism has spread since the beginning of World War I. Universal suffrage, suspension of the overseas dispatch of troops, gender equality, and protection of workers' rights were approved. In 1925, the General Election Law was enacted to allow participants to participate in elections regardless of the amount of tax paid.

At that time, the idea of the emperor as a institution in the nation was spreading. However, World War I strengthened the military and led to the idea that the emperor was not just an institution but also to be worshipped, which lasted until the end of the Pacific War.

Showa Period and Wars

After the Russo-Japanese War in 1905, the popularity of military personnel increased and the number of boys who became military personnel increased.[1] However, as the times progressed, Japan began to take a policy of international cooperation, and its armaments also shrank. As a result, the social status of military personnel declined, the morale of young officers declined, and the military became dissatisfied.

In October 1929, the stock prices of the United States plunged and the world economy was in turmoil. U.S. president Herbert Hoover tried to recover the U.S. economy by eliminating trade with other countries and colonies.[2] As a result, there were no countries Japan could trade with. Japan, which lacks resources, was in danger of collapsing. In this way, Japan had no other way to rebuild its country than to expand into Asia.

In addition, the world had a strong bias against Japan, and the United States passed a bill banning Japanese immigrants. Around this time, the circulation of newspapers increased, and these events had a great influence on the formation of public opinion in Japan.

Against this background, in 1931 the Manchurian Incident occurred when the Kwantung Army of Japan blew up the railroad tracks of the Manchuria Railway and blamed the Chinese army. Newspapers praised the Japanese military, and the people supported the troops occupying various parts of Manchuria. The Cabinet attempted to curb the military's actions, but the military ignored them, leading Japan toward militarism.

By 1932, Japan controlled Manchuria but faced international criticism for breaking the Kellogg-Brian Treaty of 1928, which was an international agreement not to use war to resolve disputes. When the League of Nations demanded the withdrawal of Japanese troops, Japan left the organization and became isolated. Military power grew in Japan, and freedom of speech dwindled. By 1936, Japan aligned with Germany and Italy, both dictatorships.

In 1937, an armed conflict between Japanese and Chinese troops broke out in the outskirts of Beijing, which eventually escalated into the Sino Japanese War. As the war dragged on, Japan was forced to focus all of its national resources and efforts on the war, resulting in significant hardships for its citizens. As a result of the prolonged conflict, the educational system underwent a transformation from elementary schools to national schools, with an emphasis on militaristic education.

In 1940, Japan formed an alliance with Germany and Italy, worsening relations with the United States. Negotiations between Japan and the US over Chinese troop withdrawal proved difficult. As Japan amassed troops near the Soviet border, the US tightened its economic blockade, causing Japan to suffer due to its heavy reliance on US oil imports. Japanese public opinion began to favor fighting the US.

In 1941, the Japanese army ambushed Pearl Harbor in Hawaii, an American naval base. Japan took military action in Southeast Asia and various parts of the Pacific Ocean and declared war on the United States and Great Britain. Subsequently, Germany and Italy also declared war on the United States, and fighting spread all over the world.

About half a year after the start of the war, Japan occupied Southeast Asia with the goal of freeing Asia from Western colonial rule, but the reality was different. The Japanese army took control and anti-Japanese sentiment increased. The people's support for the government and military increased after Japan's victory. The Japanese Cabinet encouraged people to unite in support of the war. The attack on the United States caused strong emotions, resulting in the detention of over 100,000 Japanese-Americans in U.S. internment camps.

In June 1942, Japan was defeated in the Battle of Midway and then quickly fell into a disadvantage in World War II. Although the military concentrated its production capacity on munitions, it could not keep up with the huge production capacity of the United States. The lives of the people became even more difficult. Italy and Germany surrendered in 1943 and 1945, respectively. In August 1945, atomic bombs were dropped on Hiroshima and Nagasaki, leading to Japan's admission of defeat on August 14. The war's impact was catastrophic, with about 3 million Japanese losing their lives, and 8.75 million people were impacted.

After the defeat, Japan came under Allied occupation, with the US taking a leading role. The US aimed to prevent Japan from becoming a threat again by dismantling its military and promoting democratization, including workers' rights, education, and the economy.

During the war, the emperor was deified and worshiped, but the emperor himself denied this.

After World War II, the Japanese economy was in a dire state due to the loss of military industry and productivity. There were shortages of supplies and food, leading to malnutrition and high prices. However, gradual improvements were made, and the political party cabinet was revitalized along with the promulgation of the Constitution of Japan, which helped to restore the national power of Japan.

During World War II, the two major powers that had a cooperative relationship, the United States and the Soviet Union, were divided after the war by two competing systems: liberalism and socialism. The United States, which watched the momentum of the Soviet Union, sought financial independence for Japan and provided support such as price controls.

The current Constitution of Japan dates from 1947. It includes three basic principles: "Respect for basic human rights," "Popular sovereignty," and "a peaceful nation." The Constitution of Japan was promulgated on November 3rd in 1946 and came into effect on May 3rd in 1947. Each of these dates is currently a Japanese holiday. Nov 3 is *Culture Day* and May 3 is *Constitution Memorial Day.*

In 1950, the war between the North Korean army and the South Korean army began on the Korean Peninsula. The Korean War created a booming economy in Japan as the country exported goods, and steel industry production recovered. Japan's defense capability declined due to US military intervention, leading to the formation of the Self-Defense Forces after the war.

After re-establishing diplomatic relations with the Soviet Union in 1956, Japan rejoined the United Nations. From the late 1950s, Japan experienced an economic boom due to a significant increase in exports. Various industries, including heavy industry sectors such as chemicals, petrochemicals, and automobiles, saw advancements in technology and increased capital investments. By the late 1960s, Japan had the second-largest gross national product among liberal nations.

Japan's booming economy continued, partly because of the Bank of Japan's interest rate policy. As a result, financial institutions and general companies began to invest surplus funds in real estate and stocks. As stock and real estate prices continued to rise, individuals also tried to make money on the wave.

Many people started borrowing money from banks to buy stocks and real estate. This raised prices even further.

In this way, a large-scale economic boom driven by monetary policy occurred. However, in 1990, when stock prices plummeted, real estate prices also plummeted. Financial institutions ended up holding a large amount of non-performing loans, and business deteriorated. Many people were struggling with debt.

This is known in Japan as the "Collapse of the Bubble economy." Since then, people's willingness to buy has fallen sharply, and the economy has plunged into a prolonged recession.

Heisei Period

The booming economy sank, and Japan was hit by major natural disasters. Culture and education have also changed greatly, and we Japanese have changed greatly compared to the Showa era.

The Hanshin-Awaji Earthquake and the Great East Japan Earthquake are representative natural disasters during the Heisei period. However, in addition to earthquakes, many people have been affected by volcanic eruptions and torrential rains. Regarding natural disasters, we still have many problems to solve. People in Japan were used to living a convenient and comfortable life, but once a lifeline is cut off due to a disaster, it is not only inconvenient, but it can also be life-threatening. Each of us had to figure out how to survive the few days without lifelines. People learned in the Heisei period that natural disasters are not someone else's problem.

Due to the collapse of the bubble economy, employment decreased as the economy became sluggish. Since then, people couldn't get jobs that they had always counted on after graduating from school. Especially from 1991 to 1992, this was called the employment ice age. Young people who could not find a job were in an unstable position. Due to the economic collapse and natural disasters, people want to maintain their current status rather than start something new. Marriage and childbirth increased even though people weren't asking for it.

Reiwa Period

The Reiwa period began in 2019. Japanese still suffer from economic problems and natural disasters. Also, the pandemic of COVID-19 and the war in Ukraine changed our lives. The Japanese people should now consider what we can do for world peace as citizens of the only country that has experienced attacks with nuclear weapons.

Commentary: International Cooperation

We can imagine that it is necessary to interact with people from different countries for business, education, and research under the current globalized situation. However, this is NOT easy to do. As mentioned in the above sections, countries have different cultures and customs that have been created during long historical periods. Thus, it is quite difficult to break a huge barrier to fill cultural and customs gaps between countries. In business and research, the purpose is to pursue profits and obtain logical results, and some may think that cultural backgrounds have nothing to do with it. However, we should not forget that business and research are done by stupid human beings (I think all humans, including me, are more or less stupid creatures). Sometimes, benefits and outcomes that should be based on logic depend on human emotions formed by various cultural backgrounds.

Even if the goals we want to achieve in research and business are the same, the approach to achieving these goals and the way of thinking about work differ among countries and individuals. Thus, for international collaborations, it is important to think how much cultural and custom gaps exist between us and our collaborators. If we skip such a thinking process, some misunderstanding might happen during the collaboration.

References

Information from "Nippon The Land and Its People" Author; Nittetsu Human Development. Published from Gakuseisya.

https://xn–u9j228h2jmngbv0k.com/

https://rekisiru.com/10006/2

A Brief History of the United States – by Kenneth MacLean

Introduction

The culture and history of the United States is much different (and much shorter!) than that of Japan. Points of commonality between the two countries arise from the spread of American popular culture around the world after the Second World War.

Founding

The United States was founded by Europeans who came west looking for the new world. For many years the American colonists were under British rule. The United States won its independence from the British in the War of Independence, sometimes called the Revolutionary War (1775–1783), which occurred shortly before the French Revolution (1789–1799) in Europe.

The major impetus for the colonists' break from the British was the attempt by England to place the colonies under the monetary control of the Bank of England. The British parliament passed the Currency Act of 1764, which banned the use of the colonists' paper money as legal tender in all of the American colonies. The Currency Act represented an effort to wrest control of monetary policy from colonial assemblies. That, and taxation issues represented by the Stamp Act of 1765 – "No taxation without representation" was a famous rallying cry of the colonists – prompted the Founding Fathers to issue the Declaration of Independence.

Along with the Bill of Rights attached to the United States Constitution, these documents encapsulate the ideals upon which the country was founded: personal freedom of speech and property rights, national sovereignty, limited government and limited government interference in individual affairs, states' rights, and freedom of religion. The Bill of Rights is an important document that guarantees basic human rights are inherent to every human being and come from God, not the State. This is the critical distinction between the U.S. Constitution and those of other countries, where the government can grant or restrict human rights through legislation.

Religion

The founders of the United States were mainly Christians, but many believed in the Deist principle that freedom to worship was a personal choice. There are two major religious themes that have influenced society, government, and religious attitudes within the United States throughout its history. They can be summarized as the Puritan ethic and the Pilgrim ethic. The Puritan religious strain is based upon strict adherence to religious dogma and is characterized by intolerance and fundamentalism ("fire and brimstone"). The Pilgrim ethic is a more open and inclusive paradigm that is characterized by tolerance and acceptance. These two themes can be identified throughout the political history of the United States.

According to the Pew Research Center's Religious Landscape Study,[3] the religious makeup of the United States is as follows: 70.6% Christian, 5.9% non-Christian, 22.8% no religion, 0.6% do not know.

The "religious right," composed of fundamentalist Christians and evangelicals, has been an important part of the American political landscape since the early 1980s. Most fundamentalists associate themselves with the Republican Party.

Interestingly, Americans tend to think of the "religious right" as a modern phenomenon. But one hundred years ago, a similar phenomenon called "Muscular Christianity" altered the educational landscape of the country. Prominent, conservative Protestants like President Teddy Roosevelt, influential educators and writers, all wrote in the popular magazines of the day, supporting a martial attitude, a "strenuous life," and the game of football for young college men, in order to breed "manly men" and to combat what was seen as the feminization of society.[4] The martial attitudes seen in college and professional sports in America is a direct result of this movement that reflected the Puritan religious strain in the United States, which resurfaced in a big way eight decades later in the form of the so-called religious right.

On the other hand, the Left in the United States is overwhelmingly secular and atheist. Since the pandemic in 2020, there has been increasing contention between secularists/atheists and those who believe in religion and spirituality, particularly on the issue of abortion.

Centralization vs. Decentralization

One of the most important issues in US economic history was the debate and the conflict between those who favored a national central bank, and those who were adamantly opposed, and who favored a decentralized banking system. The "central bank" theme reflected an important dichotomy of thinking within the country during the 18th and 19th centuries, between those who favored a more relaxed and decentralized agricultural life, and those who favored more centralization and industrialization. This debate began early in the history of the country, when Alexander Hamilton, the nation's first Secretary of the Treasury, pushed strongly for the establishment of a central bank that would be solely responsible for the issuance of bank notes (this was not successful). Both the First National Bank (1791–1811) and the Second National Bank

(1811–1833) issued only 20% of the nation's currency, with state banks issuing the rest.

Many of the Founding Fathers were adamantly opposed to a central bank, seeing it, as Thomas Jefferson said, as an engine for speculation, financial manipulation, and corruption. In 1833, President Andrew Jackson succeeded in destroying the Second Bank of the United States by vetoing its 1832 re-charter by Congress, and by withholding U.S. funds, for which he was censured. In 1913 the United States did establish a privately owned, national central bank, called the Federal Reserve Bank, and became the world's leading industrial power after the second world war. But the issues of centralization vs. decentralization (big government vs. small government, big banks vs. small banks) are still alive in American politics and culture today.

By 2022, the U.S. government had grown so large that it was taking over 4 trillion dollars out of the economy in that fiscal year. It seems that centralization has won out over decentralization in the US.

Western Expansion

When the United States first gained its independence, the country consisted of 13 states located along the Atlantic coast of North America. The territory of the United States was increased greatly when the United States acquired the territory of Louisiana from the French in 1803, which consisted of 828,000 square miles (2,140,000 square kilometers) of France's claim to the territory of Louisiana. This transaction is known in U.S. history as the Louisiana Purchase.

The Louisiana territory encompassed all or part of 15 current U.S. states and two Canadian provinces. The land purchased contained all of present-day Arkansas, Missouri, Iowa, Oklahoma, Kansas, and Nebraska; parts of Minnesota that were west of the Mississippi River; most of North Dakota; most of South Dakota; northeastern New Mexico; northern Texas; the portions of Montana, Wyoming, and Colorado east of the Continental Divide; Louisiana west of the Mississippi River, including the city of New Orleans; and small portions of land that would eventually become part of the Canadian provinces of Alberta and Saskatchewan.

After the Louisiana Purchase, the conceptual horizons of the young country expanded tremendously. The nation's leaders began to think of the country in continental terms. The push westward by settlers and immigrants into the west eventually created a country that encompassed land in the lower half of the North American continent from the Atlantic to the Pacific oceans. It also spawned an entrepreneurial, explorative, self-sufficient, and freedom-loving attitude that was characterized by the phenomenon known as the American West, and which has been idealized in the Western movie. This attitude is an integral part of American cultural values, and is very important in understanding American culture.

Civil Conflict

In the mid-nineteenth century, the United States experienced a massive internal conflict called the Civil War (1861–1865). The economic basis for the Civil War was the naval blockade by the North, and the political split was largely based on the issue of slavery.

The Union Navy maintained a strenuous effort on the Atlantic and Gulf Coast of the Confederate States of America designed to prevent the passage of trade goods, supplies, and arms to and from the Confederacy. Ships that tried to evade the blockade were operated by the British (using Royal Navy officers on leave).

The Civil War was also fought over the issue of slavery. The Southern stares were mostly agricultural and Democratic, while the industrial states were in the north, and were the seat of the abolitionist movement to outlaw slavery and the base for the newly established Republican party. Southern plantation owners claimed that they needed slaves in order to grow and harvest their crops.

President Abraham Lincoln was assassinated on April 14, 1865, as the Civil War was drawing to a close, the first of four assassinations of American presidents. Six other American presidents have survived assassination attempts. The War Between the States was finally won by the North, but solidified a divisive split into two factions. Even today, a subtle North-South tension exists between southerners and northerners in the United States.

Immigration

The United States is a land settled by immigrants from all over the world. Immigration has been part of the American political and cultural landscape since the country was founded.

There are five main periods of immigration to the US: the colonial period, the mid-nineteenth century, the turn of the twentieth century, post-1965, and post-2020. Each period brought different national groups, races, and ethnicities to the United States. Almost 500,000 Europeans came to America between 1609 and 1775. Many of these new arrivals were indentured servants. The first black Africans to come to America during this period also came as indentured servants. However, almost all the Africans who followed came as chattel slaves. The mid-nineteenth century saw mainly an influx from northern Europe; the early twentieth-century mainly from Southern and Eastern Europe; post-1965 mostly from Latin America and Asia.

In 2006 the United States accepted more legal immigrants as permanent residents than all other countries in the world combined. The foreign-born population of the US was 44.8 million in 2018. Since 1965, the number of immigrants living in the U.S. has more than quadrupled. In 2018, immigrants accounted for 13.7% of the U.S. population. Over one million persons were naturalized as U.S. citizens in 2008. The leading countries of origin of immigrants to the United States were Mexico, India, the Philippines, and China. Nearly 14 million immigrants entered the United States from 2000 to 2010.

In 2021 President Biden essentially opened the southern border of the US by handicapping the Border Patrol and inviting migrants in from all over the world. Migrants were seen with T-shirts that read, "Biden Let Us In."[5]

The issue of immigration, immigration quotas, and illegal immigration is, and has been, an important political theme throughout the history of the country. On one hand, periodic waves of legal immigration has led to a new vitality and energy in U.S. society, as new arrivals worked hard to "make it" and contributed greatly to society. On the other hand, illegal immigration can place great burdens on local economies and their social structure, when illegal migrants use social services but do not pay for them.

Bolstered by legal immigration, the United States was the world leader in science from the end of World War II until the end of the 20th century. Many of the electronic and computerized devices we take for granted today, for example, were first designed and built in the US. However, manufacturing has gradually left the country during the past several decades, and has shifted to Asia.

Immigration continues to be a hot-button issue in American society. Unfortunately, no one who crosses the southern border escapes the brutal Mexican drug cartels. The suffering of these migrants, who are merely following President Biden's invitation to come to this country, is depressing to me.[6]

Almost all persons who cross the border are in hock to one or the other of these criminal organizations. When migrants cross the border they are given armbands of different colors by the drug cartels – who are also trafficking fentanyl, a dangerous and addicting drug – indicating how much they have paid and how many times they have crossed.[7]

In the fiscal year 2020–21, over 1.6 million illegal immigrants flooded the U.S. southern border, from over 80 different countries.[8] This is a larger number than all of the active duty military members in the U.S. military, which is 1.35 million[9] as of 2020. In 2022 the figure was larger.

The drug cartels control large swaths of the U.S. southern border.

Isolationism

Another important political theme throughout the 20th century in the United States is the issue of isolationism. The United States has only once been invaded by a foreign country: that was during the War of 1812, when the British sacked and burned Washington DC, and damaged the U.S. Capitol Building.

Because the United States has never experienced a serious invasion of its territory since then, it has led to a feeling of self-sufficiency and a belief in the invulnerability of the country. Understanding this concept is very important to understanding the American mindset in the 20th century.

During World War I (1914–1918), the US kept out of the conflict until 1917. During WW II (1939–1945) the US did not enter the war until the Japanese aerial attack on Pearl Harbor in Hawaii, on December 7,

1941. The US has bases in at least 74 countries and troops practically all over the world, ranging from thousands to just one in some countries (it could be a military attaché, for instance). In the post WW II period, support for the American military was an important part of the fabric of American politics, American culture, and American foreign policy, and is felt strongly at the grassroots. No understanding of American culture is possible without recognizing this effect of the military on the cultural fabric of modern America.

The events of September 11, 2001 shattered the popular idea that the United States was invulnerable, and caused people in the United States to feel more insecure.

Commentary

Those who accuse the US of being isolationist don't understand the aggressive nature of U.S. foreign policy. From 1946, when the U.S. covertly overthrew the Iranian president Mossadegh and installed Shah Riza Pahlevi, the US – in the name of democracy – has overthrown governments all over the world and engaged in a series of regional wars in Korea, Vietnam, Iraq, Afghanistan, and at the time of this writing, covertly in Ukraine.

Culture

Because the United States has been settled by immigrants from outside the country, and because the US is a relatively "new" country, the people of the United States have been in general friendly and tolerant of the beliefs of others. Before the pandemic of 2020, the entrepreneurial spirit was alive and well within the US, based on a "can do" attitude that featured an optimistic viewpoint. In general, the people of the United States (as opposed to its government) are open, friendly, and tolerant. This is balanced by a fundamentalist strain, mentioned earlier as the Puritan ethic.

In contrast to Asian countries, which traditionally respect the elderly, youth and beauty are celebrated in the United States. Old age is associated with ugliness and decrepitude. A cursory examination of American TV and popular culture will easily confirm this. Most advertisements, movies, and popular music, are aimed at the young, or to those older persons who want to look younger.

In short, the cultural norms of the United States have been characterized by personal freedom, tolerance and openness, an entrepreneurial spirit, support for the US military, and a high level of creativity and desire for independence and personal freedom, which is countered by a fundamentalist and intolerant attitude within the population.

U.S. interaction with Japan

The attack on Pearl Harbor in 1941 cemented anti-Japanese feeling in the United States. U.S. citizens of Japanese descent were rounded up and placed into detention camps. However, after WW II, the United States contributed greatly to the re-industrialization of Japan, both technically and financially. In exchange, the United States demanded that US troops be stationed on Japanese soil, and has insisted on Japanese loyalty to the United States, especially during the Cold War. After World War II, the US wanted a military presence in Asia, to counteract possible aggressive actions by the "sleeping giant" of China, which was thought might become hostile to the United States. Presently, Japan is largely perceived in the United States as a peaceful country whose citizens are hard-working and honest. However, during the 1970s to the 1990s especially, there was great resentment as Japanese auto makers and electronics companies took over the manufacturing of these products from American manufacturers.

There is a certain positive mystique about Japanese culture among the general American population, symbolized perfectly by Pat Norita's character Mr. Miyagi in the popular American film, "The Karate Kid." Japanese film makers such as Akira Kurosawa ("The Seven Samurai"), and baseball stars such as Ichiro Suzuki and Shohei Ohtani, are popular and recognized personalities in the United States. In general Japan is perceived more positively by Americans than is China, even though the two countries share common cultural qualities. This has been emphasized since 2020 with the spread of COVID-19 from the a biolab in Wuhan city.

My personal reflections: Internal Civil War

Since the incident on September 11, 2001, in which the Twin Tower buildings in New York were destroyed, with much loss of life, the United States has turned inward. Draconian legislation has been passed in Congress since that incident, which has eroded personal freedoms guaranteed by the US Constitution and the Bill of Rights. The US government adopted a policy of fighting a "War on Terror," which has caused much ill-will throughout the world. Meanwhile, during the past twenty years or so, the US has become the world's largest debtor nation, a trend that has continued as of this writing. The balance of economic power has shifted away from the United States and to Asia over the past twenty years.

Unfortunately, the COVID-19 pandemic changed the cultural norms in the US, which has seen an increasing trend toward centralization of State power and dogmatism, and away from tolerance and the free exchange of ideas.[10] The 2020 and 2021 lockdowns caused economic, emotional, and psychological hardship, and have caused a cultural sea-change. Many small businesses have been forced to close, while large corporate box stores have thrived. Rioting in the streets of American cities (in 2020) caused many Americans to doubt the validity of our political and economic institutions. Younger people have been disenfranchised by an economy that was shut down, and a financial system where interest rates were so low (until 2022) that saving was almost illogical. Combine this with a rigid, permanent, political and medical bureaucracy (see the testimony of former CDC commissioner, Dr. Robert Redfield, before the U.S. Congress)[11] and the result is a combination of apathy, despair, and anger among many in the U.S. population.

In July 2022, the assassination of Shinzo Abe, the former Japanese Prime Minister and serving member of Japan's House of Representatives, created shock waves throughout Japan and the US. Through all this, formal inter-governmental relations between Japan and the United States remain friendly as of this writing.

Chapter 1 Notes

1. (page 12) The Russian-Japanese war was a brief military conflict in which a victorious Japan forced Russia to abandon its expansionist policy in East Asia, thereby becoming the first Asian power in modern times to defeat a European power.

2. (page 12)

On June 17, 1930, President Herbert Hoover signed the Hawley-Smoot Tariff Act, which dramatically raised import taxes on foreign goods. This led to a major disruption of world trade and substantial economic hardships in other countries.

3. (page 20)

https://www.pewresearch.org/religion/religious-landscape-study/

4. (page 21) See Martin Radermacher, 2017, "Evangelicals and the Body," in *Devotional Fitness. Popular Culture, Religion and Society, A Social-Scientific Approach,* vol 2. Springer, Cham., at https://doi.org/10.1007/978-3-319-49823-2_5

5. (page 25)

https://www.snopes.com/fact-check/immigrants-biden-shirts-let-us-in/

6. (page 26)

See the Law and Border show, at

https://americasvoice.news/playlists/law-and-border/ for in-place reporting of the situation.

7. (page 26)

Mexican drug cartels issue colorful wristbands to identify migrants who have paid them for passage across the Rio Grande, how many times they have tried to cross, and who is eligible to cross again if they've been sent back, a South Texas lawmaker's office confirmed to Border Report on Thursday. "In the RGV area, the Gulf Cartel controls the alien smuggling groups. The various alien smuggling groups issue bracelets to each alien being smuggled into the U.S.," the office of U.S. Rep. Henry Cuellar, a Democrat who represents this area, told Border Report. "Bracelets are different colors because aliens get three chances to cross successfully for one price. First time crossers get red bracelets. If unsuccessful, they get another color. Aliens receive purple bracelets when it's their last chance to cross," Cuellar's office said in an email to Border Report. "The wording represents who has paid and who still

owes money for the smuggling."
Source: Sandra Sanchez, "Colored wristbands help cartels tracks migrants, payments for smuggling them, lawmaker confirms," at https://www.borderreport.com/immigration/border-crime/exclusive-colored-wristbands-help-cartels-track-migrants-payments-for-smuggling-them-lawmaker-confirms/

8. (page 26)

https://www.pewresearch.org/fact-tank/2021/11/09/whats-happening-at-the-u-s-mexico-border-in-7-charts/

9. (page 26)

https://usafacts.org/state-of-the-union/defense

10. (page 29)

See the Twitter Files at https://jordansather.substack.com/p/running-list-of-all-twitter-files

11. (page 30)

See Dr. Robert Malone, "Dr. Redfield's Bombshell Testimony," at https://www.theepochtimes.com/health/dr-redfields-bombshell-testimony_5112580.html

—2—

The Lives of Two Common Citizens: Taro Yamada and Robert Smith

The Life of Taro Yamada – by Nobuhiro Suzuki

April 20, 1977

Taro was born on April 20, 1977, in Tokyo. During the early 1970s, Japan was in the midst of significant economic growth. It was also a milestone year for environmental problems, where the pollution problems due to economic growth became apparent in various negative ways. It was also in the early 1970s that the Cup Noodle was released from Nisshin, and the first McDonalds opened in 1971 at Ginza, Tokyo. These events may have triggered a major change in the Japanese diet.

In 1973, a shortage of gasoline and paper products due to the first oil crisis caused a flood of panicked, hoarding customers in supermarkets to buy bathroom papers! Prices soared, and the collapse of the high-growth policy became clear. In addition, many companies went bankrupt. However, Taro's family was not really affected by the first oil crisis because his father was working for a huge company. Taro's mother was a housewife.

Like any other baby in Japan, Taro's parents took him to a Shinto

Shrine for a Japanese traditional ceremony, named "Miyamairi," 31 days after his birth. This is the ceremony to express gratitude to a god, "Ubuno-kami," for the birth of a baby, and to have a shrine priest pray for his health and happiness. Ubuno-kami is believed to protect the person from before birth until after death. Many rituals related to gods called "Shinji" are performed at shrines. Also, about 100 days after birth, milk teeth start to grow. At this time Taro also had Hyakunichi-Iwai, a ritual to imitate eating with the wish that "the baby will not have trouble eating for the rest of life."

April 1, 1981

Taro started kindergarten. Unlike the US, the new semester starts in April in Japan. Taro's father was working in a company and his mother was a housewife. In this situation, the majority of kids go to kindergarten. However, if both father and mother are working, it is hard for parents to take care of their kids. In this case, children go to a nursery center instead of to kindergarten.

This was the first time Taro stayed a long time with many other kids. In Japan, there are many kindergartens that are related to Buddhism or Christianity. However, many Japanese are flexible about religion, so kids in a Buddhist family can also go to Christian kindergarten. It is more important that the kindergarten is close to the home.

Nov 15, 1981

Taro was 5 years old (east Asian age reckoning, real age 4 years old). His parents brought him to a Shinto shrine again for the ceremony called Shichi-Go-San. This is an event for three- and seven-year-old girls and five-year-old boys, held annually on November 15 to celebrate the growth and well-being of young children.

Why is this ceremony held at the ages of 3, 5 and 7 years old? It is different depending on the region (Shich, Go, and San mean 7, 5, and 3, respectively).

April 1, 1984–March 31, 1990

Taro began elementary school on April 1, 1984 and graduated on March 31, 1990.

Just before going to elementary school, his grandparents bought him a Randoseru, a special school bag for Japanese elementary school. Randoseru is a backpack made of stitched firm leather or leather-like synthetic material. (Probably, some Americans know Randoseru, because in the Japanese animation, Doraemon, one of the main characters, Nobita, has a Randoseru when he goes to school.)

Taro felt that it was a really big present for him. Also, he started abacus lessons. At that time, learning abacus was one of the most popular lessons for kids (now it is not).

Taro was doing relatively well studying in elementary school. But, the most favorite time in the school was the school meal. (As of 2004, 99% of elementary school students and 82% of junior high school students eat a school lunch). However, Taro did not like the time of cleaning. In Japan, a student's duty is to clean their own classroom. Taro was not cleaning very well, and sometimes his teacher was really upset about it.

When Taro was going to elementary school, the economic bubble started. The whole of Japan was full of money, and many people enjoyed a luxurious life. Many people believed that this situation would last forever.

April 1, 1990–March 31, 1993

Taro became a junior high school student. In the school, students are required to wear the "Tsume-eri" style uniform. This style has a collar that is worn by closing it with a button or hook up to the neck. Taro and other students did not like it. It looks like an old army uniform.

In Japan, students begin to study English in class. Taro was interested in learning it because he imagined that he would be able to speak English when he graduated from junior high school.

Unfortunately, in Taro's generation, English was an important subject for entrance exams for high school, not for communication with people from other countries. Thus, he was not able to speak English when he graduated.

Taro started to play Kendo as a club activity. Kendo is a traditional martial art in which players fight using bamboo swords while wearing protective clothing. In Japan, most students start club activities in junior high school. Club activities may be efficient for many kids to learn the concept of "Senpai" (senior) and "Kouhai" (Junior). In Japan, people are taught to respect older people.

Taro studied hard in junior high school, because he needed to go to a high ranked high school. In Japan, to get good job opportunities, people should go to a high ranked high school, then a high ranked university. In Japan, hard educational competition begins in junior high school (currently it is getting earlier). Taro wanted to go to a top ranked private high school.

However, the economic bubble ended and it impacted the company of Taro's father. The company did not go bankrupt, but the economic situation of Taro's family changed. Unfortunately, Taro needed to go to a public high school with a lower tuition.

April 1, 1993–March 31, 1996

Although Taro needed to give up going to a private high school, he succeeded in entering one of the highest ranked public high schools. In high school, educational competition to go to a good university is getting harder, so some students stop club activities or start an easier activity compared to that in junior high school. During the economic bubble it was easy for young people to find jobs, but that situation ended.

Taro needed to study hard to go to a high ranked university. Taro gave up Kendo. (A few years later, Taro experienced an era of difficult employment called "the Employment Ice Age.") Taro was aiming to go to the University of Tokyo, the top ranked public university in Japan.

During his high school life, Japanese society was suffering from huge destructive incidents. In January 1995, a massive earthquake with magnitude 7.3 attacked the Kansai area (around Kobe and Osaka). The damage to the urban areas of Kobe City near the earthquake source was enormous. The number of victims reached 6,434, which is the second largest earthquake disaster that occurred post-WW2, after the Great East Japan Earthquake in 2011.

In March 1995, members of the cult movement Aum Shinrikyo caused the Tokyo subway sarin attack. It was a rare, indiscriminate terrorist attack that used chemical weapons in metropolitan areas.

April 1, 1996–March 31, 1997

Unfortunately, Taro failed to enter the university which he wanted to go. In Japan, some students go to prep school for at least one year to study for university entrance exams. Taro studied like crazy and finally succeeded in passing the exam to enter the University of Tokyo.

April 1, 1997–March 31, 2001

Taro began his university life, and started a new club activity. Also, he started a lot of part time jobs. He enjoyed his university life with a lot of parties. Was he very busy? Yes! Because of so many activities, Taro stopped studying. He had been studying so very hard and made it to the University of Tokyo, so he thought that he did not need to study hard anymore. Indeed, when Taro was a high school and prep school student, his parents, his teachers in high school and in prep school told him, "You are studying very hard, but you will be free from studying in the university." Such a situation is common for Japanese students. For Taro's generation, universities were paradise! Taro needed only a minimum amount of study to earn credits. It was enough for him.

Taro was a junior in the university from April 1, 1999. Most of university students start job hunting in the autumn of their junior year (if they do not go to graduate school). In Japan, almost all students doing job hunting wear a suit of the same color (navy blue), and a tie. We call such a suit a "recruit suit."

In Japan, all students not going to graduate school need to get a job offer before graduation. If they fail to do so, their life may go into "hard mode."

As mentioned above, after the end of the economic bubble, it became hard for young people to find a job. Taro also suffered from such a situation.

In Japan, people who were born between 1970–1984, and graduated university around 2000, were called the "generation of the Employment Ice Age."

Taro was trying to find a job in a large and famous company, but he only got a job offer from a small company.

September 15, 2008

The majority of people felt that the Japanese economy was not really good. But the company where Taro worked was doing well because of its IT business with the US. Taro had plans to be married on Sep 20, 2008.

However, the bankruptcy of Lehman Brothers (Japanese call it the "Lehman shock") occurred on Sep 15. Taro's company, which was doing business with the US, was dramatically affected. Business with the US stopped and some staff became the target of restructuring.

Fortunately, Taro was not targeted. But, in order to rebuild the company, Taro needed to work like crazy for the company. Taro had to change his life plans. He postponed his marriage.

The Lehman economic incident affected not only Taro's company, but also many businesses in Japan. In Japan, after getting a job in a company, the majority of people work for the company until their retirement at 60 years of age. Unlike in the US, it is not common in Japan to change jobs for career progression. However, such a working style has been changing recently. The bankruptcy of Lehman Brothers was likely one of the triggers for this change.

March 11, 2011

The bankruptcy of Lehman Brothers dramatically changed the Japanese economy. However, an even more serious incident occurred in Japan. All Japanese people will never forget it.

A terrible earthquake occurred in east Japan. In Fukushima, the nuclear power plant was destroyed by a tsunami and a meltdown of the nuclear reactor occurred. However, the power company hid this fact. Thus, people were confused without accurate information. Everyone knew that radiation leaked from the power plant and spread to the surrounding area, including Tokyo, but people did not accurately know how much the radiation affected their life and health. So much information was transmitted – both correct and incorrect – via SNS (social networking services) on TWITTER and FACEBOOK. Some mass media fueled fear.

Of course, this incident affected Taro's life in Tokyo. Tokyo also suffered from a huge earthquake, and public transportation was completely stopped. Many people were not able to go back home just after the earthquake. Many people went back home by walking for several hours. Taro needed to stop working for several days.

Taro's fiancé was afraid of the effects of radiation, especially during rainy days. Relatively high levels of radioactivity were detected in areas where rainwater collects, such as puddles. Many people in Tokyo considered evacuating to western areas, where the effects of radiation may have been less than in eastern areas. However, Taro and his family decided to stay in Tokyo. He did not have any family or relatives in the western area of Japan.

This incident was a "turning point" that changed the lifestyle of Japanese. Disaster countermeasures have been strengthened throughout Japan.

June 15, 2012

Taro married the lady (who was working in the same company) when he was 35 years old. Thirty-five is later than the average Japanese marriage age. In Japan, the age of marriage is getting older. Also, the number of people who will not marry is increasing. Traditionally, people marry in their 20s or early 30s. Thus, Taro's parents tried to push him to marry when he was in his late 20s.

In Japan, marriage is a big event not only for individuals, but also for families. Traditionally, the oldest son is the heir to the family. The marriage of the oldest son is very important to keep the family strong. In many cases, therefore, the oldest son has a responsibility to take care of the house and the tombs inherited from older generations. Taro did not like such old ways of thinking.

Ideally the son, not the daughter, is the heir to the family. So, after the marriage, Taro's parents started to push him and his wife to have kids (sons are better). Actually, this is a very old way of thinking. However, some people still follow these traditions (although fewer and fewer Japanese are doing so).

2021

Taro is still working in the same company. When he was a small child, he (and probably others) thought that he would have a "normal" life just like his father. He feels now that his life is very different from what he thought back then. It might be because of the dramatic events, such as the economic bubble, the bankruptcy of Lehman Brothers, the eastern Japan earthquake, and COVID-19.

From July to September 2021, the Olympic and Paralympic games were held in Japan, despite the opposition of many Japanese people. Taro enjoyed watching some sports on TV. However, he worried about the future of Japan.

Now, Taro thinks about his son's future. His son does not need to think about being the heir of the family. However, his son may still need to struggle with studying for the entrance exams.

In addition, Taro worries about the economic situation, because Japan currently holds more than $10 trillion in government bonds ($10,000,000,000,000!). The Japanese people really need to think about how Japan should be changed and what should be unchanged.

Conclusion

I have described Taro's life as a typical Japanese man born in 1977. Of course, the life of the Japanese people is diverse. In addition, it should be noted that the lifestyle of Japanese people is always changing in line with the times. However, Japanese people may be more uniform, compared to people in the US. Also, some Japanese people are still bound by traditional thinking about "family."

These characteristics of the Japanese people may be formed by history. Therefore, it is important to know Japanese history to understand the Japanese (see Chapter 1).

Yearly Cultural Events for Japanese

January 1–New Year's Day In Japan, New Year's Day is the most important holiday. Many companies are commonly closed during the first three days of the new year, the period called "Sanga nichi" or "Shogatsu." The first visit to a temple or shrine in the new year is called "Hatsumode." There are many different traditional events in each home.

The second Monday of January – Coming-of-Age Day It is a national holiday (in Japanese "Seijin no Hi"). Each city, town, and village holds a congratulatory ceremony. In Japan, the age of majority is 20. According to Japanese law, people can start to drink alcohol and smoke tobacco when they reach the age of 20.

February 3 or 4 – Setsubun (not a holiday) Setsubun is the day before the beginning of spring. You may think it is far from the beginning of spring. But this is because Setsubun is derived from the old lunar calendar.

On Setsubun day, people normally do “Mame-maki” in the evening. People throw away beans and say, “Devils out! Happiness in!” And people eat the number of beans that match their age.

February 11 – National Foundation Day It is a national holiday where the founding of Japan as a country is celebrated.

February 14 – Valentine's Day (not a holiday) In Japan, it has become from some sweets company's sale strategies. However, it has become established as a day to give chocolate from women to men, and a wide variety of rules unique to Japan that are different from those overseas.

February 23 – Emperor's Birthday The Emperor's Birthday is a national holiday. By the way, when the new emperor took the throne in 2019 the era changed from “Heisei” to “Reiwa.” Each Japanese emperor's reign is given a name, or ”Gengo,” that is then used alongside the Western calendar to mark the years.

March 3 – Hina Matsuri (not a holiday) Hina matsuri is the Festival of Dolls for girls. People celebrate the health and happiness of girls and display “Hina Ningyo,” which means Hina dolls. They represent the imperial court wedding of the Heian period. These are not dolls for girls to play with because they are ornamental items to decorate the house.

Around March 21 – Vernal Equinox Day This is a national holiday. A week consisting of three days before and after the vernal and autumnal equinox days is called ”Higan.” Many people go to the family grave and make a Buddhist memorial service for their ancestors.

April 1 – An entrance ceremony is held in Japan In Japan, the new fiscal year for many things – including the start of school – begins on April 1. In elementary schools without uniforms, students wear suits. The entrance ceremony is attended mainly by mothers, not busy fathers. Mothers attend in kimono or suits. The entrance ceremony is held in junior high school and in high school in new uniforms. At the entrance ceremony of the university, it is done in the same way, wearing a suit. Of course, either parent will attend.

The company entrance ceremony is also on the same day. The "entry ceremony" where new employees meet together is said to be a "strange practice" in the world. It seems that this ceremony does not exist outside Japan. Even with the unique Japanese custom of recruiting new graduates all at once and employment rather than employment.

April 29 – Showa Day Originally, Showa Day was the Emperor's Birthday during the Showa Period. After the change to Emperor's Birthday during the beginning of the Heisei Period, this holiday remained as Greenery Day (see below) to keep Golden Week. Then, it changed to Showa Day in 2005.

May 3 – Constitution Memorial Day It was enacted to commemorate the enforcement of the Constitution of Japan on May 3, 1947.

May 4 – Greenery Day Greenery Day was named "National Holiday." There is a law called the Holiday Law in Japan, and weekdays between holidays also becomes a holiday. Greenery Day moved to May 4 in 2005.

May 5 – Children's Day ("Tango no Sekku") Since the Nara period, the birth and growth of boys has been celebrated ("Tango no Sekku"), and Children's Day was decided to be on May 5th during the Edo period.

The day when many people raise the carp-shaped streamers is called "Koinobori" in Japanese. Just as the "Hina matsuri" decorates special dolls for girls, the "Tango no sekku" decorates the house with "Kabuto" and "Yoroi," or May dolls, for boys. They are considered a symbol of strength and vitality.

The period of four national holidays, Showa Day, Constitution Memorial Day, Greenery Day, and Children's Day, and weekends and holidays is called "Golden Week." It started in 1951 when a movie company named this period the "golden period" and advertised it. This period is on the same level as the New Year.

3rd Monday of July – Marine Day Marine Day was established in 1996 as a day to thank the blessings of the sea and wish for the prosperity of Japan, a maritime nation.

August 11 – Mountain Day Mountain Day was established in 2016 as a day to thank the blessings of the mountain and wish for the prosperity of Japan, a mountain nation.

3rd Monday of September – Respect for the Aged Day Respect for the Aged Day originated from an event held in a small village in Hyogo prefecture. It was an event that was opened in 1947 with the purpose "to cherish the old people and build a village with the wisdom of the elderly." This concept spread throughout Japan and this holiday was established in 1966.

Around Sep 22 – Autumnal Equinox Day See Vernal Equinox Day. This is also a day when the lengths of day and night are equal.

2nd Monday of October – Sports Day Sports Day was originally established in 1966 as a memorial holiday for the opening ceremony of the Tokyo Olympic Games (older one).

November 3 – Culture Day Culture Day was enacted in 1948 as a memorial holiday in which the constitution of Japan was promulgated.

November 23 – Labor Thanksgiving Day This day originated from the event "Niinamesai," dedicating the harvest of the year to God and to thank him for a good harvest the following year. It was established in 1948 as a national holiday to "work hard, celebrate production, and thank each other."

December 24 and 25 – Christmas Eve and Christmas (not a holiday) In Japan, Christmas is not a holiday. In the USA, it is an important holiday in which family members stay together. However, in Japan, it is a day for dating of young couples. It is good day for children because Santa Claus and parents will give them a good present. In addition, it is also a day to eat Kentucky Fried Chicken.

December 31 – New Year's Eve On New Year's Eve, a temple monk rings a bell called "Joya no kane" 108 times. It is said that there are 108 worldly desires per person. Every time the bell rings, one of the 108 worldly desires is erased, and the desire to spend a happy year next year is included.

Most of the Japanese people eat buckwheat noodles. We call this noodle "Toshikoshi Soba." Because noodles are long, people eat soba for good luck and healthy longevity.

Japanese clean up the whole house at the end of the year (it should be done by December 31). During the Edo period, it was customary to set December 13 as the day of soot removal to prepare to welcome God. This is said to be the origin of this custom.

The dates of some holidays in Japan is flexible because of the Happy Monday system. It is a law revision that moves some of the national holidays from the conventional fixed days to Mondays of a specific week in Japan.

The Life of Robert Smith by Kenneth MacLean

The 1950s

Robert Smith was born in Detroit, Michigan on November 13, 1951. Robert's father was a policeman and his mother was a housewife. During this time Detroit was the center of the world's automobile industry. After WW 2 the United States entered what could be called a golden age. At one point the US was producing fully 50% of the world's industrial output. Because of the dominance of the U.S. economy in the world after World War 2, the U.S. dollar became the world's reserve currency.

And so Robert grew up in an environment where almost everyone had a positive outlook for the future. In Robert's working class neighborhood, all of the children asked themselves, "What do you want to be when you grow up?" This question is significant because neither the children nor their parents questioned whether it was possible to be anything that was desired: an airline pilot, a teacher, an engineer, a barber, a policeman, a nurse, an office worker, or even the President of the United States.

During this time, the 1950s, there was a feeling in almost every part of the country of unlimited opportunity. The economy was rapidly growing and expanding.

Robert was baptized Catholic and attended church every Sunday until he went to high school. Robert's father was a practicing Catholic.

Robert was introduced to rock and roll in the late 1950s by his father.

1960s

When Robert was 10 he joined the Boy Scouts. Adults took city kids out to the country where they would camp in the woods, learn to fish and hike, and canoe. Robert's father taught him to use a bow and arrow. In Robert's neighborhood there were lots of kids, who got together and played pick-up baseball games at the local baseball field. Robert's father put a backboard and a basket over his garage. Robert played pickup half-court basketball games with some of the neighbor kids. Robert's hands were too small to properly grip the basketball so he abandoned that activity in high school. Football was too violent for Robert, who was a tall skinny kid. Robert was coordinated, but not an athlete. He was too slow to seriously play sports. Robert used to skate with neighborhood kids in the winter at an ice rink made by one of the neighbors on an open lot. Robert joined a junior hockey team, but he wasn't a good skater. His hockey coach once told him, "Son, if you could play hockey standing still, you'd be the next Gordie Howe." (Gordie Howe was one of the most famous professional hockey players of all time.)

In the 1960s, Robert, like most kids in Detroit, listened to the rock stations and followed the "Top 50" pop music charts, and bought 45 and 33 vinyl records. Robert also listened to Barry Gordy's Motown, an African American company that produced hits that went all over the country, and the world. Robert discovered jazz music in college, listening to the student radio station at the University of Michigan, which produced a lifelong love affair for Robert with this music. During this time the Civil Rights movement was in full swing. Robert saw race riots at his high school, and experienced the Black Action Movement at U-M, which closed down the university for a semester, and was the forerunner to the Black Lives Matter movement. Robert also attended many demonstrations against the Vietnam War, and saw social unrest that resulted in property damage.

Robert grew up during the Cold War, an insane time for people of all ages. When Robert was in grade school, drills were routinely held in school in case of a nuclear attack from the Soviet Union. Children were taught to go under their desks and cover their heads. A macabre joke during that time circulated among the students that described these drills: "Put your head between your legs and kiss your ass goodbye."

This was nothing, of course, to the fate of the citizens of Hiroshima and Nagasaki in 1945, when primitive nuclear weapons were detonated on those cities, killing tens of thousands of civilians. In the US, this is rarely talked about. Some argue for its necessity to end the war. Others say it was an unnecessary and barbaric act of mass murder. Regardless, these incidents were seared into the consciousness of the world. The fact of "mutual assured destruction" from nuclear bombs was the basis for arms limitations agreements, beginning in 1959 with the Antarctica Treaty, to the 1968 Non-proliferation Treaty, all the way to the New Strategic Arms Reduction Treaty in 2010.

Robert attended Carleton grade school from first grade to sixth grade. Carleton was a public school. Robert often walked a mile to school every day and back, or rode his bike. Robert learned not to fear the weather, or the cold, or snow. Sometimes he rode the school bus when the weather was very bad. Just before Robert went to 7th grade his parents moved across the street from St. Clare de Montefalco school in Detroit, so he attended 7th and 8th grade at this Catholic school. Robert's teachers were all nuns, who dressed in the traditional black and white garb. (Most Catholic nuns now do not wear this clothing). The chain the nun is wearing is called a rosary, a set of prayer beads that Catholics use to say their daily prayers.

From 1965–1969 Robert attended Finney high school, a public school. Robert was interested in every subject, and entered a pre-calculus class to prepare for college. At this time college entrance exams were very important. Robert was not a good test taker and only scored moderately well. However, at that time the University of Michigan expanded its enrollment and Robert was able to squeak in. He found himself in a huge dormitory with hundreds of other students from all over the country, and many from other countries.

1969–1973

Between 1969 and 1973 Robert attended the University of Michigan, one of the best public universities in the country. He was interested in politics, philosophy, economics, and also math and science. Robert eventually majored in political science after taking economics, philosophy, math, chemistry, and physics courses.

At that time the competition at the school was so intense that Robert got only passing grades in his STEM courses. He realized that he would not be able to be a scientist, so he chose a different major: political science. Robert thought that there might be a scientific basis for understanding human events.

Robert soon learned that this idea was a fantasy. The more he studied political science and observed world events, the more he realized how messed up the world was. Robert took the Foreign Service exam, but did not do well enough to qualify.

Robert remembered his father warning him about college during the summer of 1969. "Those liberals in Ann Arbor will warp your mind," he said. "Soon you will be doing drugs, you won't be going to Church anymore, and you'll become a communist."

Truer words were never spoken!

During his college days Robert experimented with drugs, and had a couple of bad experiences. In his dorm there were two known drug suppliers, where kids could literally get anything except heroin and cocaine. On the fifth floor at Alice Lloyd Hall in 1969–1970, marijuana, hashish, and any number of psychedelics were readily available.

One of the very first things Robert did (to spite his father) was attend a Communist Party meeting on campus. Robert was fascinated with concepts like the class struggle, the primacy of the working class, the anti-war sentiment, and the idea that communism would bring about a socialist utopia for all people. (At that time the US was engaged in the Vietnam War. All of the media in the US was rigidly conservative and pro-war.) After the Communist Party meeting Robert bought Mao's Little Red Book at the local campus drug store in 1970, as did many other students.

Robert had a good laugh reading this book, which he considered to be a collection of unabashed nonsense. Robert studied Marxism-Leninism and found it equally ridiculous, promoting idiotic concepts like the "dictatorship of the proletariat." When Robert examined the societies in communist countries, he saw that they were all totalitarian dictatorships with failing economies. Equally bad were the right-wing military dictatorships in Africa, Asia, and South America.

So, although Robert defied the dictates of his father, he soon learned through experience the danger of drugs and the emptiness of social systems like communism and fascism. This didn't prevent him, however, from attending anti-war rallies. Robert learned from his college days a healthy skepticism for authority, and stupid political systems on both left and right. Robert became an iconoclast, determined to think for himself and not fall prey to ideologues and dogmatists on both sides of the political spectrum.

However, Robert never attended church again, which was a constant sore point with his father until his death in 2005.

1973

After college Robert had no interest in working in the corporate world. He did not relish being "a cog in the machine," a sentiment expressed admirably by John Lennon in his song, "Mr. Nowhere Man." During his post-college years Robert became disillusioned with the world. His university studies, and his reading on spiritual subjects, showed him that the human race really didn't know where it was going. There was a randomness and a destructiveness in human affairs that no one could explain. Robert became an independent home services contractor, working in the trades as a house painter. Robert enjoyed this work, for he was a physical person who liked running and playing sports. His working class background saw nothing wrong with this work, for he knew he was helping people in a very practical way, even as all of Robert's friends became professionals: computer programmers and engineers.

Robert had always been interested in spiritual subjects after his mother died of cancer when he was 3 (she was only 28 at the time). When he walked up to her casket and saw her body lying there he wanted to know why she didn't get up and hug him. This experience began a lifelong interest in spirituality.

1978

In 1978 Robert married Jennifer, his soul mate and lifelong companion. Robert's marriage has been a rock upon which his life has been based.

In a sense Robert's life began to differ from the norm after he left college. Robert got married but had no children, in contrast to the "typical American" who had children, raised families, took their sons (and daughters) to baseball and football games, drove them to hockey and football and soccer practice, made them do their homework, participated in Parent-Teacher meetings at the local school, and imbued their children with a sense of optimism about the future.

Commentary

For many people of all classes and ethnicities, the typical American believed in what I call "the American Spirit." I will let a Cuban immigrant to the US speak to this. I got this from an anonymous poster in a comment section:

> No one ever talks about how Cuban-Americans contribute to our beautiful America. We have adopted this great country's culture by: opening businesses and hiring, eating good ole country food, voting, paying our taxes, buying boats, cars, waving the American flag, buying American music, standing up for the anthem, and on and on…even my uncle chose to be buried in an American flag t-shirt with a native American holding an eagle. As soon as we step foot into this country, we learn to quickly respect and love it. Of course, there are some bad apples amongst us that give us a bad name some times, but that's in any culture. Cubans have always aspired to become as American as any black, native, or white man. We

> love and cherish this great country. In school, I am always the only Cuban, at work I am always the only Cuban, anywhere I go, I'm usually the only Cuban, but in my heart I'm probably the most American and appreciate the red, white and blue til' death because it loved me more than my own blood in Cuba. My own government, my own blood, pushed us out. God bless America and 'viva Cuba libre'!

This sentiment expresses the view of many people who can be called conservative.

Others, mainly those who live in big cities and college towns, see the history of the US as a series of terrible blunders, both domestically and internationally. Particularly, many city dwellers see the endless wars America's military provoke and fight in smaller countries all over the world, and see America's corporations as greedy capitalists who care only for profit and nothing for humanity.

Robert sees the truth on both sides, but he is a tiny minority. After the 2016 election in which Donald Trump beat Hillary Clinton, opinions have hardened, and Americans are at each others' throats on social media.

1988–1994

The computer revolution was in full swing in the 1990s. Robert bought one of the first personal computers, a Commodore 64, and began to program on it.

During these years Robert attended part-time classes at a local community college, and later went back to school part time at Eastern Michigan University, majoring in computer science. However, Robert turned out not to be such a great programmer. He found himself getting headaches staring at the screen when programming, and abandoned his plan or being a programmer, continuing with his work in the trades.

In 1991 Robert and Jennifer moved out of Ann Arbor to a small rural neighborhood next to a large piece of farmland. He did almost all of his work for people in the city. He worked for people of all races and social classes, from university professors, corporate CEOs, non-U.S. citizens, and people who lived in trailer parks.

In order to get jobs he had to meet new people every week. Even though Robert is a loner, he had to sell himself and learn how to talk with people he had never met before. This was very helpful, for Robert learned a diversity of opinions.

Robert discovered the value of being humble, and never bought into the superior attitude of those who thought that (as Hillary Clinton said) working class people who voted for Trump were "deplorables."

In fact, working class people build the homes and fix the appliances and keep the world running.

2000

After the silly "Y2K" scare, in which the entirety of Western civilization was supposed to collapse because of the dating system in the world's computers, Robert concluded that the mass media in the United States was largely engaged in fear-mongering and the promotion of narratives. He learned to be skeptical of "news cycles," which promote the latest scare.

Robert began writing metaphysical books and science fiction novels with a spiritual bent. He also investigated three dimensional solids called polyhedra, and wrote a geometry book with a mathematical analysis of some important polyhedra. During this period Robert became a freelance editor of academic journals, books, and novels.

2016–2021

In America prior to the election of Donald Trump in 2016, a sense of tolerance, friendliness, and respect for others was a common theme among the middle class. America has citizens from probably every country in the world. We are a nation of immigrants, and have learned to tolerate opposing views and cultures. Although African Americans are only 12% of the U.S. population, which is still majority Caucasian, U.S. voters twice elected Barack Obama as president of the country.

Although Robert did not vote for Trump in 2016, he was amazed when he saw the headline in the Washington Post on the very first morning of Trump's presidency, January 20, 2017: "The campaign to impeach President Trump has begun."[12]

All Robert knew about Trump was his TV show, "The Apprentice," which Robert thought was pretty dumb. On the other hand, why was the mainstream media in a frenzy about this guy? Being an iconoclast, the "establishment's" constant criticism of the man during the campaign almost persuaded him to vote Republican, which he had never done since he became a voter (that changed in 2020).

Of course the opposition party wants to win the next election, and the Post is a very liberal publication, but Robert understood that for the next four years the political battle was going to heat up. And it did! Trump was impeached twice during his term as president, and the political schism in the US hardened considerably.

COVID-19 – 2020 – Present

The schism hardened even further during the COVID-19 pandemic, which has changed cultural norms in the US and has led to suppression of free speech that does not toe the central government's line.[13] Robert, through his studies of Marxism-Leninism, sees an eerie resemblance of the current political landscape in the US to Mao's Cultural Revolution (1966–1976).

2023

In February of 2023, whitehouse.gov published a statement in February 2023 that announces the intention of the U.S. government to give the World Health Organization *carte blanche* control over the country's medical system. A health emergency can be declared in Geneva, allowing health authorities to issue diktats that violate a country's sovereignty and constitution. (https://www.whitehouse.gov/briefing-room/statements-releases/2022/02/02/fact-sheet-the-biden-administrations-commitment-to-global-health/)

For Robert, this development is a logical progression of those who favor the centralized form of human organization (see Chapter 6).

Commentary

The United States was founded as a constitutional republic. The states are the laboratories of democracy. The U.S. central government itself is a creation of the states. Unfortunately, the central government in Washington DC has devolved into a corrupt caricature of the intention of the Founders, ruled by a permanent political class that has been bought off by the country's wealthy corporations, who write the laws that are rubber-stamped by a Congress mired in political confrontation and rhetoric.

Nevertheless, America's civil society has been and is still stable and strong, developed from a large middle class that arose after WW 2, and the belief by the majority of working class folks that they too could eventually own a house, raise a family, and improve their standard of living. This belief has inspired millions of immigrants to come to the US. In contrast, no one is getting on a boat or a plane to immigrate to totalitarian societies. People of all races routinely flee from these degraded, mismanaged countries, even as the US is accused of being "systemically racist" by persons who have no understanding of tolerance or compassion for others. In Robert's opinion, these atheists and materialists have no spiritual understanding and no conception of their higher connection to the Creative Source.

The "Typical American"

The "typical American" does not exist because of the tremendous diversity of cultures. Each culture and race has its own story. But for Robert Smith, the American spirit is not dead yet. Even as privileged U.S. elites on Wall Street, wealthy corporate CEOs, narrow-minded intellectuals and academics, a partisan corporate-controlled media, and the permanent political class revile the United States as a hopeless failure, people all over the country are waking up to the valuable cultural attributes that are still the backbone of American beliefs about itself.

Robert shares these beliefs as well.

Yearly cultural events for Americans

January 1 Americans begin the year on January 1 by celebrating New Years day. This is a federal and national holiday. In Robert's house this was usually spent watching American football games. Families often gather to celebrate together.

February 14 St. Valentine's Day, or Valentine's Day, has become a significant cultural, religious, and commercial celebration of romance and love in many regions of the world. Americans exchange heart-shaped cards or romantic tokens on this day. This is not a national holiday, so people still have to work, but it is nationally recognized.

March 17 St. Patrick's day is a cultural and religious celebration held on the traditional death date of Saint Patrick, the foremost patron saint of Ireland. For Americans, this holiday is essentially a drinking holiday, because in America the Irish have a reputation of being heavy drinkers. People gather in bars and restaurants and drink alcohol (or they did before COVID-19). A popular Irish joke goes:

"Did you hear about the three Irishmen who left the pub before it closed?"

"It could happen!"

On a Sunday in March or April Easter is the principal festival of the Christian church, celebrating the Resurrection of Jesus Christ on the third day after his Crucifixion. Easter follows Lent, a period of 40 days observed by acts of penance and fasting. Traditionally, parents decorate and/or color the shells of hard-boiled eggs and hide them for children to find. This is called an "Easter egg hunt." The "Easter bunny" is the symbol of Easter Day. The Easter Bunny is a folkloric figure and symbol of Easter, depicted as a rabbit—sometimes dressed with clothes—bringing Easter eggs.

End of May - Memorial Day This holiday is celebrated on the last Monday of May. It is a federal and national holiday in the United States for honoring U.S. military personnel who have died in the performance of their military duties. Traditionally it is the beginning of summer in America. Family and friends get together, barbecue, drink, and play sports.

July 4 – Independence Day A federal and national holiday that celebrates the signing of the Declaration of Independence of the United States, on July 4, 1776. On that day the Continental Congress declared that the thirteen American colonies were no longer subject to the monarch of Britain, King George III, and were now united, free, and independent states. On this day Americans hang flags and get together for barbecues, play sports, go to the beach, and do many summer activities.

Early September – Labor Day This national and federal holiday is celebrated on the first Monday in September to honor and recognize the American labor movement and the works and contributions of laborers to the development and achievements of the United States. In America it is the start of the school year.

October 31 – Halloween This is not a national holiday but is celebrated throughout the country. It began as a day dedicated to remembering the dead, including saints (hallows), martyrs, and all the faithful departed. Now it is a PARTY DAY! Americans dress up in crazy costumes, and children "trick or treat," going around the neighborhood and getting candy and sweets from the neighbors. This holiday is so big that temporary stores pop up in many cities selling costumes, candy, and prank toys. The big stores always have a section dedicated to Halloween.

End of November – Thanksgiving Thanksgiving Day in the United States is celebrated on the fourth Thursday of November each year. Traditionally it is a time to give thanks for all the sacrifice and hard work done for the harvest. This is a family day. Turkey is usually served for the main meal, and family sit around the table talking. In Robert's house, the men usually watch the nationally televised American football games and the women talk.

December 25 – Christmas Day A national and federal holiday, this is another family day. Sometimes friends of the family are also invited for a big celebration, and a big meal is often served. Many people get the time between Christmas and New Years Day off from work.

Chapter 2 Notes

12. (page 56)
https://www.washingtonpost.com/news/post-politics/wp/2017/01/20/the-campaign-to-impeach-president-trump-has-begun/
13. (page 56)
See the Twitter Files at https://jordansather.substack.com/p/running-list-of-all-twitter-files

— 3 —

The US – Japan Relationship

How Can People in the US and Japan Get to Know Each Other Better? – by Nobuhiro Suzuki

We are writing this chapter because, to know each other better, it is important to learn the history, culture, and everyday life of another culture. It sounds very simple, but is difficult. If we could do this easily, all conflict would be gone. Therefore, we should think about why it is difficult to know the history, culture, and lifestyle of another nation. One reason may be that people who say, "I know about (US) (Japan)" just think they know.

Fortunately, many people in the US and Japan can access the internet relatively easily to get information about other countries. However, we should also know that we may have biases when we search for information using the internet. In that case, we are searching for what we like, not what we should know. Many people are obtaining information about only a small part of another country.

The best way to understand each other is to live in another country. However, even if the Japanese (or US) people live in the US (or Japan), we should know that we are living in a small part of the country. I lived in Reno, Nevada for more than five years and moved to Denton, Texas. I lived there for almost four years. However, I still feel that I do not fully understand the culture of the US. In the US, cultures and even laws are different depending on the state. People in South Dakota and Texas don't know each other.

Also, we don't know everything about our own countries. In Japan, we learn the history of Japan from elementary school to high school. However, as entrance exams in Japan are very hard (please see Chapter 1), many Japanese students try to memorize history to get good scores on their entrance exams. Consequently, many Japanese forget Japanese history after the entrance exam. Although Japan is a very small country when compared to the US, cultures and dialects are very different depending on the region. When Japanese try to talk in each other's dialect, the language may not be understood. In addition, another problem in Japan is that many people, especially young people, are not interested in politics. Voter turnout even for very important elections such as the elections for the House of Representatives often drops to a bit above 50%. In this situation, it may be hard for Japanese people to really understand what is going on in Japan.

How can we know about other countries without knowing our own country?

We now have more opportunities to use online tools such as Skype or Zoom to interact with people from other countries. It is likely that before the pandemic, many people rarely used such tools. Also, some people have greater opportunities to interact with people in other countries. Fortunately, many people now know that these tools are available for international exchange. Thus, to know about other countries, it should be very important for us to flexibly adapt to new environments, or changes in the world situation.

The most important thing to know, in my opinion, is that human beings are basically stupid. Human beings still continue to war, our activities highly impact the natural environment, we still try to fool others and are blinded by the power of money,.... We know these are not good, but we are so stupid that we can't stop. We know that we are basically stupid, yet we continue to think, "O.K. we are the most intelligent species on the earth and have the ability to understand each other."

How two mortal enemies in WW II became friendly nations

It may be impossible for us to completely understand each other. However, full understanding may not be necessary. The USA and Japan, two mortal enemies in WWII, became friendly nations, perhaps because these countries are not similar. Countries with different cultures can complement each other's lack or weaknesses. For Japan, the leadership of the USA and the diligence of the Japanese may be really a good combination to achieve high economic growth. In fact, the Japanese have a history of working desperately under American leadership to achieve postwar reconstruction. Also, the Japanese characteristics of social harmony have been helpful for good relations with the USA. In addition, after WWII, many Japanese had a longing for America's leadership and tried to emulate the American lifestyle.

I think the Americans may have respected the diligence of the Japanese. The development of Japan after the war may have surprised Americans and changed Americans' views of the Japanese. Probably, the relationship between the USA and Japan was not a sudden one, but one that was gradually formed by mutual respect.

How Can People in the US and Japan Get to Know Each Other Better? – by Kenneth MacLean

The best way to know and understand a culture is to live there, learn the language, and interact with people from that culture. However, that is only possible for a very small fragment of the population.

Modernly, people learn about other cultures via mass media, social media, cultural events, and movies and entertainment. Chat software allows people in any country to talk to others in another country. The only limitation on this form of communication is the desire to do so. The barriers to communication between people in the US and people in Japan have largely been eliminated.

The biggest mistake for those who cannot travel to the US is to try to understand the American people via its mass media and social media.

A half-century ago, media in the US was more local and decentralized. Three major networks, ABC, NBC, and CBS, dominated national news coverage. However, local newspapers and radio and TV stations had their own cadre of reporters and broadcasters, who emphasized local issues and brought a local slant to national news coverage. As this video demonstrates, the local coverage of national issues has mostly disappeared in the United States. Local news outlets are largely just talking heads who echo the "spin" of the national news networks, whose coverage is synchronized.[14]

In the US today, journalists push narratives, not information.

The point is, learning about America from watching American media is a futile exercise. Social media is no better. The country is completely polarized, largely around one figure: Donald Trump. Trump has not been president since January 2021, yet the mainstream media news is either pro-Trump or anti-Trump on many issues. Donald J. Trump lives rent free in the heads of almost every American. Unbelievably, *Psychology Today* recognizes a psychological condition called TDS, which stands for "Trump Derangement Syndrome."[15]

The Trump phenomenon – a divisiveness and a preoccupation that borders on obsession – may be an offshoot of what psychologist Prof. Mathias Desmet calls "mass formation psychosis," (MFP), which is associated around the world with the lockdowns and forced vaccinations mandated by many of the world's governments in relation to COVID-19. In a nutshell, MFP occurs when a society is overcome by fear and discontent (COVID), and is exacerbated when people are separated and lack social bonding (lockdowns). When society also experiences what Prof. Desmet calls a "lack of sense-making," (events have no definitive causation and seem to have occurred senselessly), mass phenomenon can emerge. In Prof. Desmet's words:

> So: meaning, anxiety, and discontent that is not connected to a specific representation. So it needs to be in the mind without the people being able to connect it to something. If you have these four things—lack of social bonds, lack of sense-making, free-floating anxiety, and free-floating psychological discontent—then society is highly at risk for the emergence of mass phenomenon. If this free-floating anxiety is highly present in a population, and the media provide a narrative, which indicates an object of anxiety, and at the same time, describe a strategy to deal with this object of anxiety, then all the anxiety connects to this object and people are willing to follow the strategy to deal with this object, no matter what the cost is. That is what happens in the beginning of mass formation.
>
> Then in a second step, people start a collective and heroic battle with this object of anxiety. And in that way, a new kind

> of social bond emerges and a new kind of sense-making. Suddenly life is all directed at battling the object of anxiety and in this way, establishing a new connection with other people. And that, the sudden switch of a negative state, a radical lack of social connection, to the opposite, to the massive social connection that is experienced in a crowd. This sudden switch leads up to a sort of mental intoxication. That's what makes mass formation, or crowd formation, the exact equivalent of hypnosis.
>
> All people who have been describing, who have been studying, mass formation, such as Gustave Le Bon, for instance [William] McDougall, [Elias] Canetti have remarked that mass formation is not similar to hypnosis; that mass formation is exactly equal to hypnosis. Mass formation is a sort of hypnosis.
>
> What happens is that at that moment, when people experience mental intoxication, it doesn't matter anymore whether the narrative is correct or wrong, even blatantly wrong. What matters is that it leads up to this mental intoxication. And that's why they continue to go along with the narrative, even if they could know by thinking for one second, that it is wrong. That is the central mechanism of mass formation. And that makes it so difficult to destroy it. Because for people, it doesn't matter when the narrative is wrong. And what we try to do is we all try to show constantly that the narrative is wrong. But for people that's not what it is all about. It's all about the fact that they don't want to go back to this painful state of free-floating anxiety. [16]

A schism in U.S. society has formed regarding COVID, the vaccine, free speech, and Donald J. Trump. Competing narratives black out information from "the other side," because adherence to a narrative makes sense of events (even if the narrative isn't science- or data-based) and prevents you from sliding back into a state of anxiety. Over time, these narratives become facts to those who support them because they are used over and over.

Each side is convinced (or determined) that their side is correct, and the other side is wrong. In conditions where mass formation is present, pseudo-science and propaganda largely replaces the free flow of information, particularly as regards medicine and the medical bureaucracy.

I say this merely as a prologue to better understand what is happening in America. Perhaps by the time this book is published a more sane normalcy will have been established.

The question is, "How can people in the US and Japan get to know each other better?" The short answer is to avoid U.S. mass media and social media, and to get together physically or in online chat groups.

Being aware of mass formation makes it easy to spot this phenomenon socially.

I have noticed that MFP is like a mask, or an overlay, to a person's true personality. Getting to know someone here in the States requires that one recognize the overlay of acquired beliefs or narratives, and reach the real person underneath the mask.

It would be absurd to suggest that everyone in the US is suffering from MFP.

However, MFP does acutely manifest itself on social media and in the news media, and in discussions about politics or current events. You may see it if one of the memes or tropes from a competing narrative is brought up in a group.

Someone may become "triggered" when one of these memes is presented, because it threatens the overlay that protects them from the fear and the senselessness.

Once you familiarize yourself with the narratives on both sides, you can spot the mask, get underneath it, and hopefully have a real conversation.

Interestingly, many arguments, even on subjects like COVID or vaccine mandates, will eventually devolve to pro-Trump or anti-Trump. ("You probably voted for Trump!" is something I see a lot on social media when someone wants to accuse another of being irrational.)

Donald J. Trump is apparently the human avatar, or representative, of a national schism in the United States.

Because the US is such a heterogeneous society, fragmentation is much easier to accomplish here than in a more homogeneous nation like Japan. Of course Japan has its own ethnic groups and cultures, but the United States is, and has always been, a nation of immigrants with sometimes radically different cultures, religions, and belief systems.

However, despite the fragmentation, I have noticed a coming-together of different races and cultures within both opposing groups. These multi-racial and multi-cultural coalitions may eventually harmonize around a socially accepted set of data points.

This would be a positive mass formation. Not a psychosis, but a broad agreement on a set of accepted and positive societal norms. As of this writing, we are a long way from that.

Fortunately, both the US and Japan have representative democratic governments, which provide common ground between the two cultures. The Japanese tendency toward social harmony makes resolving societal conflicts in Japan easier than in a free-booting United States with its emphasis on individuality.

How two mortal enemies in WW II became friendly nations

It all began in 1854. An American fleet of warships, under the order of U.S. president Millard Fillmore, and commanded by Admiral Perry, forced the Tokugawa Shogunate to sign the Treaty of Peace and Amity. This treaty was the end of the Edo period in Japan, which had lasted for 220 years. The Edo period was an era of national seclusion (sakoku) dominated by the Shogunate.

The U.S. involvement with Japan in World War 2 began with the Japanese bombing of Pearl Harbor on December 7, 1941. Immediately after the war, the United States was determined to neutralize the Japanese military. Through the aegis of General Douglass MacArthur, the US imposed a constitution and a government on Japan that established a Western-style democracy with Japanese characteristics. The Japanese military was essentially eliminated, and Japan's economic and political systems were rebuilt. After 1949, the US saw democratic Japan as a counter to Mao's brutal Communist dictatorship in China.

Japan took full advantage of the military protection given by the US, and, unlike Germany after World War 1, revitalized its economy and built a peaceful, prosperous society. The primary reason for why the US and Japan became friendly nations is, in my opinion, largely because the Japanese people are a more homogeneous and harmonious society compared to the United States. Japan took a rational approach to their defeat in WW 2 and decided to go with the flow, accepting U.S. help and building a market oriented society that is also socially responsible.

Credit also goes to the US, who did not crush a smaller nation, but oversaw a rebuilding process that gave independence to a country defeated in war. The post-war U.S. policy toward Japan, in my opinion, was partly due to a feeling of guilt after the horrific atomic explosions on Nagasaki and Hiroshima, in which tens of thousands of civilians died.

At the time of this writing, both countries are concerned with the government in China, led by the Chinese Communist Party (CCP), which has broken its agreement with the UK regarding Hong Kong, and has overturned the democratic process there. The CCP is also threatening to invade Taiwan, another free society with a democratic government. Cuba, a few miles off the coast of Florida, has signed an agreement with the CCP to participate in their Belt and Road program. This is an eerie reminder to the US of the Soviet placement of nuclear missiles during the Cuban Missile Crisis of 1962, when war tensions between the two nuclear powers were high.

A strong relationship between the people and the governments of Japan and the US is vital to maintain peace in the entire South and East China Sea area. The South China Sea has tremendous economic and geostrategic importance because about one-third of the world's maritime shipping passes through it. As of 2017, the area carries over US $3 trillion in trade every year. It is important, therefore, for these two democracies to remain united and work peacefully together as the CCP, under the leadership of Xi Jinping, becomes more aggressive toward other nations in the area. Japan and the United States must continue their strong and successful relationship.

Chapter 3 Notes

14. (page 65) See https://www.youtube.com/watch?v=hWLjYJ4BzvI and https://www.youtube.com/watch?v=TM8L7bdwVaA

15. (page 66)

See “Is ‘Trump Derangement Syndrome’ a Real Mental Condition?” at https://www.psychologytoday.com/us/blog/talking-about-men/201901/is-trump-derangement-syndrome-real-mental-condition

16. (page 67)

From the website zero-sum.org, “Mass Formation (Psychosis) and the Coronavirus Narrative,” Interview with Prof. Mattias Desmet by Reiner Fuellmich and the Corona Investigative Committee, at https://zero-sum.org/mass-formation-psychosis-and-the-coronavirus-narrative/#close

—4—

The 2020 U.S. Election – An Inflection Point

Note: This chapter is included because of the overwhelming importance of the 2020 presidential election in the US, which is still a hot political topic in my country.

Before the 2020 U.S. Election – by Nobuhiro Suzuki

The "hidden Trump faction" never "expresses support" From https://gendai.ismedia.jp/articles/-/76422?imp=0: In Japanese. This article is typical of Japanese sentiment.

Why so many people don't say what they really mean

The article discusses the uncertainty surrounding the outcome of the 2020 U.S. presidential election, with attention focused on whether Biden or Trump will win. The author notes that recent news about the alleged connection between the Biden family and Ukrainian energy companies may impact the election, and that there may be a significant number of "hidden Trump supporters" who do not openly express their support until election day. The article cites a survey indicating that 77% of Republicans are reluctant to say who they support, compared to 52% of Democrats and 59% of Independents. The author explores the psychology behind this phenomenon and why some Trump supporters may choose to keep their support hidden.

I don't know what will happen if I express my support for Trump

The article discusses the sensitivity of political discussions in the US and Japan, where politics can sometimes create tension and discomfort in relationships. It suggests that the fear of being rejected or suppressed by those with opposing views could be why some voters don't openly express their political beliefs. The article also explores the idea of "hidden Trump supporters" and how expressing support for Trump can sometimes result in social exclusion and personal safety concerns. The author suggests that there is a growing issue of intolerance towards different perspectives and ideas in America, which can lead to social problems.

The author spoke to Joe Sanders, a 72-year-old acquaintance who enjoys discussing political topics, regardless of his own opinion. The author notes that while Americans have fought hard for their freedom, many people now struggle to tolerate different perspectives and ideas, leading to attacks on opposing ideologies by radical groups. The author suggests that this is becoming a social problem, with some people hesitant to speak out for fear of becoming a target for these groups, especially in urban areas where they are concentrated.

The article also describes how expressing support for Trump can sometimes lead to breaking friendships and family relationships, endangering personal safety, and even facing discrimination at schools. The author shares an anecdote about a friend who was told to exclude Trump supporters from his social circle and mentions a Dear Abby column where parents asked if they should keep their child away from relatives who support Trump.

Comments from Nobu

The article said that "hidden Trumpers" want to vote for Donald Trump, but cannot tell it to others, because they may be involved in serious trouble. Unfortunately, Trump supporters and anti-Trump people are always fighting.

In the USA, people with different (even totally opposite) opinions can debate about anything without hating each other. Actually, it is much more difficult to do this in Japan. I think it significantly contributed to the establishment of the USA and made this country the best leader in the world.

After reading the article, I thought the USA has totally changed. For me, one of the best cultures, the USA, started to be ruined. Many people, including me, cannot predict what will happen in the world, or in the USA, after this election. For me, it is relatively easy to imagine that this situation may continue after this election whether Donald Trump wins or not.

Of course, it is very important whether Donald Trump wins or not. However, it is also important (I say even more important) how the world will change depending on the results of this election.

In the previous chapter we described the difficulty with international collaboration. However, from the news, I feel that it is also difficult to understand each other even among people living in the same country.

After the 2020 U.S. Election – by Nobuhiro Suzuki

Is Biden's "Victory" in the US Presidential Election Positive for the Japanese Economy?

https://www.newsweekjapan.jp/kaya/2020/11/post-120_1.php

Wednesday, November 11, 2020 12:01

The article discusses the impact of the Trump administration's economic policy on Japan and the international community, and the changes that may come with the arrival of the Biden administration. Trump's policies, which prioritized nationalism over free trade, have disrupted the traditional role of the US as a global leader. If the US continues down this path, the world may become divided between the US, China, and Europe, which would have significant implications for Japan.

The author argues that Japan, which has benefited greatly from free trade, will need to adapt to these changes and may need to reconsider its alliance with the US. This is the opinion expressed by many in Japan.

The article discusses the potential economic impact of the 2020 U.S. presidential election on Japan. If Trump is reelected, tax cuts will continue, but the trade war with China may intensify, leading to a decline in Japan's exports to the US. In contrast, Biden plans to invest in renewable energy and manufacturing, but stock prices may initially fall due to tax increases. However, consumption by the middle class will recover in the long term, leading to sustainable growth. Regardless of who wins, Japan should consider transitioning to a domestic demand-led economy to avoid being affected by U.S. isolationism.

Comments from Nobu

I am not a specialist in politics and should not say what's going on in the world, even in Japan. However, I guess that self-centeredness might not function because no one can stop globalization. Too many things have already been connected by the internet all over the world, and such a trend will be accelerated in the future. Thus, in the current situation, almost all countries including the US and Japan need to consider the effects of this election on the entire world, not only in their own countries. We need to be flexible so that we can adapt to the dramatic changes in the world.

Before the U.S. Election – by Kenneth MacLean, Ann Arbor, MI USA, October 17, 2020

A cursory analysis of the upcoming U.S. election would show that the political debate in the US is an argument between Left and Right, centered around Donald Trump. But this is a very limited perspective. The election is really about the form that a global society will take during the rest of this century.

Do we want an efficient, centralized global control system that is not so much concerned with different perspectives as it is with the efficient moving of products and services around the globe? Or do we want to live in a more decentralized system that is based around the nation state and allows for diversity of cultural and national points of view, but which may be more argumentative and inefficient? The decentralized system allows for personal freedom but may involve more conflict between various groups. Even more unfortunately, the centralized, globalist economic model comes with a ubiquitous surveillance state and social credit systems that treat human beings like apps. Dissent and conflict are suppressed by internal police or government forces that also suppress alternative ideas.

Behind the craziness in the US is this debate, but almost no one recognizes the larger issue. The real choice in the US is between corporatism/globalism and populism.

The U.S. election will likely not be over on Nov 3. Lawyers for both sides will challenge the votes in every state that doesn't go their way. The Electoral College meets to cast their votes on December 14. On January 6, 2021, the votes are counted and verified in a joint session of Congress. If no candidate receives 270 electoral votes, the election will be decided in the House of Representatives in a one-state-one-vote process.

After the Election – by Kenneth MacLean, April 14, 2021

Charade: A game in which the players are typically divided into two teams, members of which take turns at acting out in pantomime a word, phrase, title, etc., which the members of their own team must guess.[17]

The election charade in the United States has now reached absurd and dangerous proportions. Call me an election denier if you want, but massive electoral fraud in six swing states has been documented by analysis of the voting in Pennsylvania, Georgia, Michigan, Nevada, Arizona, and Wisconsin. The Smartmatic and Dominion voting machines were used to alter votes from Trump to Biden, employing the strategy of "Drop and Roll."

See https://www.youtube.com/watch?v=1_P3-Z2MV5I

After the polls closed at 11p.m. on November 3rd, Trump had big leads in Michigan, Pennsylvania, and Wisconsin. By noon the following day, those leads had magically disappeared. The chairman of the U.S. Federal Election Commission, Trey Trainor, has stated, the "massive amounts of affidavits that we see in these cases show that there was in fact fraud that took place. And the other side really needs to answer these questions."[18]

Here is one example of voter fraud in Pennsylvania (there are too many sources to list here). Trump gets 19,958 votes subtracted from his tally, while Biden gets 19,958 votes added to his tally. You can't lose votes if the election is being counted fairly.

See https://populist.press/dominion-caught-red-handed-stealing-votes-on-live-tv/

The absurdity has gotten so bad that a lawsuit was filed in Wayne County, stating that the Trump Campaign is "racist" because it is exercising its legal and constitutional right to challenge electoral fraud in Wayne County, Michigan.

Cars and vans with out of state license plates were filmed trucking in ballots to the vote counting center in Detroit after the polls closed on November 3rd. The center was closed at 4 a.m., and poll watchers were told to go home. By noon Trump's over 100,000-vote lead in Michigan had gone to Biden. Similar events occurred in Milwaukee, Wisconsin, and in Pennsylvania.[19]

The political machines in America's large cities have been engaging in voter fraud since at least 1960, when the Daley machine in Chicago flipped Illinois to JFK, the Democratic candidate, who beat Richard Nixon, the Republican candidate. Nixon's campaign told him that they had proof of fraud in Chicago and that he could challenge and probably win the 1960 election, but Nixon decided to move on. (He later won the presidency in 1968 and again in 1972).

The reasons behind the election charade in the US goes back to my previous essay, "Before the Election." The U.S. election is representative of a world-wide contest between competing methods of organizing human societies. The globalist/corporate business model with totalitarian, centrally planned economies using state capitalism with low wages favorable to the balance sheets of multinational corporations – the business model of the Chinese Communist Party and America's business elites, who have joined forces – competes against a diverse and decentralized system where nation-states voluntarily cooperate with each other in a global setting, and where individual freedoms and liberty are guaranteed by free and fair elections and the rule of law.

The media in the US are largely just propaganda outlets for each side. This is partially a result of what Professor Matthais Desmet calls the mass formation phenomenon, which produces a sort of hypnotic attachment to narratives, on both sides of the political fence, regardless of the rationality of those narratives.

The first step in restoring balance to the US is a thorough analysis of voter fraud accusations by the Republicans. If Joe Biden is serious about uniting the country, he should be cooperating with Republicans to show Americans that Trump's accusations of voter fraud are false. All that is necessary is an inspection of the voting process and an analysis of the voting machine images. Auditing each vote (comparing ballots to voter rolls and signatures) will easily determine if votes are valid or fraudulent, and prove once and for all whether the accusations of Republicans and Trump are fake.

Updates

As of September 2022, there has been no "official" investigation of these charges (but many unofficial ones), which continues to needlessly perpetuate them into the future. Those who do investigate are called "election deniers" by the media. Every court that has handled one of the election fraud lawsuits has dismissed the case on technicalities before a single piece of evidence could be heard. My hope is that the U.S. Supreme Court will eventually hear a combined lawsuit and settle this question once and for all.

As of October 2022, most of the voting machine records of the 2022 election have been erased in many U.S. counties. By law, these voting records must be maintained for 22 months after each national election. This date has now expired. A last-ditch effort by citizens was made to retrieve the 2020 cast vote count from each of the over 3,000 counties in the US. This effort resulted in over 800 county records retrieved, and a preliminary analysis shows voting irregularities in 96% of the counties.

Of course there are voting irregularities in all U.S. elections. The extent of these irregularities is the question. Was there enough error to overturn Biden's slim margins in the six swing states? This has yet to be determined as of this writing. The Trump side has stated – irrationally, many say – that they will not stop until all voting records from the 2020 election are retrieved. This is probably not possible now.

A more rational vote-counting system should be implemented in the US, following the example of France. In France, voting machines have been outlawed and all votes are on paper ballots and counted by hand. Ballots are place in transparent plastic cylinders at all polling places so that anyone can see if mischief is being done. All votes are counted in the polling stations and the count process is open to the public. The results of national elections in France are announced across the country by midnight at the end of the voting day.

In my opinion, this system is too simple and rational for the US. Here, tensions are so high that reasonable solutions are immediately rejected!

However, the accusations of fraud – Hillary Clinton also accused the Trump side of voter fraud in 2016, and warned about voting machine irregularities prior to the election – have galvanized voter sentiment on both sides. Paradoxically, this led to a huge increase in voter turnout and in mail-in votes during the November 2022 mid-term elections.

To conclude, the entire 2020 election revolved around one person: Donald J. Trump. The opposing candidate, Joe Biden, hardly bothered to campaign. The 2020 U.S. election wasn't Trump vs. Biden, it was pro-Trump or anti-Trump. I find this to be a depressing state of affairs for my country. Throughout the Biden administration the main topic of conversation has been and continues to be Donald Trump! The recent report released by the Biden administration about the disastrous withdrawal of U.S. troops from Afghanistan in September of 2022 blamed Trump. This is crazy. Trump hasn't been in power since January of 2021.

Just before this book was published, on April 4, 2023, Trump was indicted, arraigned, and fingerprinted in New York City on charges that even many in the charging party feel are weak. The other political party is convinced that this action was politically motivated. The arrest of a former president on what are essentially bookkeeping charges has never occurred in U.S. history because it sets a dangerous precedent for detaining officials after they have left office, or even while in office, for purely political purposes.

There is a curse that says: "May you live in interesting times," which is used ironically to point out that in prosperous periods, more harmony exists and life is easier. Here in the US, events are occurring with such rapidity that it is almost impossible to follow the news cycle. I believe that in the US we are approaching a denouement that will hopefully resolve a lot of the built-up social and economic tensions in my country.

Chapter 4 Notes

17. (page 79)

From Dictionary.com, definition of "charade."

18. (page 79)

https://justthenews.com/politics-policy/elections/federal-election-commission-chairman-trump-campaign-bringing-legitimate

19. (page 80)

See https://nationalfile.com/video-unmarked-containers-rolled-into-secure-detroit-voting-center-at-4-am/

— 5 —

The 2020 Pandemic

5.1 The Covid-19 pandemic and changes in the workplace environment – by Nobuhiro Suzuki

In Japan, it has always been important how many hours we work per day, or how many days we work per week. Approximately 30 years ago in Japan, there was an energy drink (like "Monster Energy" or "Red Bull") named "Regain." The TV commercial for it said, "Can you fight "work" for 24 hours a day?" In Japan, it is important to stay in the office or working place as long as possible. In some cases, the amount of work or the time spent working is considered to be more important than the quality of work. (This is true; I am not kidding.)

I feel that, in Japan, people have a strong consciousness that we should work for the same company. Many people want to work in different jobs for their company. For example, someone who worked in the office of human resources will move to the office of accounting in the same company. Such a relocation can occur frequently. In Japan, if you ask someone, "What is your job?", many people will answer, "I am a company employee."

Recently, the consciousness of younger people about work started to change. I feel that the change has become even greater due to the pandemic. Many people learned that we can work from home and that we should change our way of working. However, in Japan, changes in the working style are still in a transitional period. Some companies are trying to take almost everything completely back to the situation before COVID-19. Moreover, some people feel the need to work more because they are working at home. Before the pandemic, almost everyone (depending on the type of job) was working in an office, and went home after finishing work for the day. Under the pandemic situation, the mode of work dramatically switched. For some people it is difficult to switch from "working" mode to "relaxing" mode when they are working at home. In schools, the rules for pandemic measures are always changing, and teachers and professors still need to work to set up for new styles of teaching.

5.2 Collaborating with people in a diverse group locally, nationally, and internationally – by Nobuhiro Suzuki

Japan is an island country geographically isolated from other countries. Yes, Japan is really close to Korea and China. However, we still need to use airplanes or huge ferries to go to these countries. As mentioned in Chapter 1, people in Japan are highly cooperative. Therefore, everyone equally followed the protocols for the prevention of COVID-19 infection. Even prior to the pandemic, Japan was considered one of the cleanest countries in the world (we can drink tap water almost everywhere in Japan). Indeed, to prevent infection by cold, many Japanese people wore masks to prevent catching a cold even before the pandemic of COVID-19. Probably, this is one reason why the number of people affected by COVID-19 is relatively lower than in the USA. On the other hand, Japan may be one of the hardest countries to come into from other counties because of Japan's pandemic measures. People from other countries must stay in a hotel for several days to make sure that they are not infected by COVID-19 (but the rules are always changing). During their stay in the hotel, they cannot even go out of their room! Such situations may make it much harder for Japanese to interact with people from other countries, and have consequently lowered the infection rate. In addition, some foreign students needed to give up studying in Japan.

Online tools such as Zoom and Skype make it easier to interact with people from other countries. These tools are also utilized for meetings with people in other regions of Japan. Therefore, some people made their domestic or international community bigger during the pandemic. For others, the pandemic made the barrier of interaction with others larger.

5.3 The Covid-19 pandemic and changes in the workplace environment – by Kenneth MacLean

Much has been written about how the 2020 pandemic has forced people out of work, or into working from home. Some businesses have set up centers where workers can do their jobs in controlled environments with social distancing and other workplace rules that limit personal contact. A lot has been written about this "modified" workplace environment, so I will not go into it here. If you have a white collar job you understand very well how COVID-19 has changed your life.

I am much more interested in the blue collar worker. You know, the people who keep the infrastructure of the world up and running. Blue collar workers are the backbone of any economy. These are the people who build the houses, repair the appliances, install and fix furnaces during cold winters, put the new roof on your house, put in that new water heater or water softener system, build affordable housing, prepare food for supermarkets and restaurants, and who grow the crops and distribute them all over the country. Not to mention the frontline healthcare workers like nurses and technicians, and EMTs, who do vital work.

I am a writer and editor, and sit at my desk most of the day. But I also work in the trades. Frankly, the world can do without my writing and editing, it can do without the journal papers and books I edit for academia, but it can't do without those who keep people from starving or freezing.

Even during the lockdowns in my city (Ann Arbor) blue collar contractors in vital industries were, by necessity, active. When I needed a new water heater in February 2020, I was able to secure an installer. When I needed a completely new water treatment system in January of 2021, a local contractor came out and did it. People still came to my house to deliver stuff I really needed.

There's a story behind this. My water system installer, who is 25 years old, did the entire job himself. He hauled my old system out, put a new one in, re-plumbed everything. As he was hauling my new equipment downstairs (backbreaking work) he said, "I'm 25 but I feel like I'm 50." Yup. That's how it works for blue collar workers, who keep the world running.

The change in workplace environment due to the pandemic has been far more beneficial for white collar workers than for independent blue-collar contractors, and employed blue collar workers, for these people must work on-site. Many white collar workers worked from home and still got paid, but many working class people lost their jobs. Middle class, working entrepreneurs such as restaurant owners and other small businesses also lost their businesses, placing them at the bottom of the economic ladder, or dependent on government subsidies to keep their families afloat. COVID-19 has eviscerated the working class and hurt the middle class, while the businesses of big corporations have prospered.

As of September, 2022, according to the Daily Mail, 4.8 million illegals have come to the U.S. southern border since January 2021, when the Biden administration changed border policy and opened the southern border to low wage, unskilled immigrants. This is great for multinational corporations, who want more cheap labor to keep wages down and profits up. However, this policy negatively affects working class Americans of all races, for bottom-wage immigrants will compete with workers who are already struggling, further depressing wages for working class people. White collar workers will be largely unaffected, for low-wage, unskilled workers don't threaten their livelihoods.

It is interesting that in 2005, Barack Obama said,

> We simply cannot allow people to pour into the United States undetected, undocumented, unchecked, and circumventing the line of people who are waiting patiently, diligently, and lawfully to become immigrants in this country.[20]

He also said,

> When it comes to immigration, I have actually put more money, under my administration, into border security than any other administration previously. We've got more security resources at the border – more National Guard, more border guards, you name it – than the previous administration. So we've ramped up significantly the issue of border security.[21]

Republicans criticize Democrats for doing what they have previously done, and Democrats criticize Republicans for doing the same things they have done in previous administrations. Important issues were and are largely ignored, such as unchecked illegal immigration, enormous government overspending, and changes in the workplace and its effect on workers due to the COVID-19 lockdowns, school closings, and vaccine mandates. That is because U.S. news is dominated by political narratives and both political parties are in thrall to corporate interests.

5.4 Collaborating with people in a diverse group locally, nationally, and internationally – by Kenneth MacLean

During the pandemic between early 2020 and the end of 2021, lockdowns and forced separation made it difficult to collaborate in person with groups of people. Social media platforms such as Twitter, YouTube, Facebook, Instagram, and a host of other online platforms became more and more valuable, allowing for the free exchange of ideas.

However, these Big Tech platforms began to censor (and still do) content related to Sars-Cov-2 and the vaccines, so these social media spaces were not appropriate for unfettered cooperation and collaboration to advance and create knowledge in fields of study, many of which have been unduly politicized. Opposing viewpoints were labeled as "disinformation" and "misinformation," driving free thinkers away.

Prestigious scientific journals got involved in politics and published fake science, said NBC News, talking about a medical study retracted by the Lancet: "'A first-year statistics major could tell you about major flaws in the design of the analysis,' one expert said."

In 2020 Bruce Y. Lee, in Forbes, said the following:

> One of the things that's truly been unprecedented is the number of prestigious scientific journals that have taken clear stances for the upcoming (2020) U.S. Presidential election. For example, Science, The Lancet, and the New England Journal of Medicine have all now urged voters not to re-elect Trump as President, as I have described previously for Forbes. Scientific American and Nature have both gone one step further and en-

dorsed Democratic challenger and former U.S. Vice-President Joe Biden for President.

When prestigious medical journals (or any scientific journal) get involved in politics, there is an obvious problem with the politicization of science. Why are these journals prestigious? Because they (in the past) have published only the most rigorous peer-reviewed studies, without bias.

Scientific opinion should be relegated to social media or political journals. Fortunately, peer-review can still be accomplished in non-traditional settings, bypassing the orthodoxy and/or bias of "accepted" journals or publishers.

The internet has shrunk the world. People have lots of experience now with various social media platforms, and there is really no distinction now between local, national, or international news. A development in the Ukraine will receive more media attention here in the US than the environmental disaster in East Palestine, Ohio, where the burning of tons of vinyl chloride set off a toxic mushroom cloud of chemicals that spread for miles, polluting air, land, and rivers.

Effective collaboration between intelligent persons must avoid the censorship of ideas. Here in the US, government, politics, and social media are contentious, and make people feel hesitant to express their ideas, or forward theories or science that disagrees with the accepted line. Therefore, effective collaborations by scientists and laypersons have become more and more ad hoc, gathering people interested in the free exchange of ideas on private platforms and alternative media. The Substack platform is a great example of brilliant minds finding an idea space that does not suppress information.[22]

In conclusion, the only requirement for effective collaboration is the ability to freely exchange ideas and original work. That is dependent on non-interference by suppressive governments, biased journals, or censorious Big Tech / Big Media companies.

Chapter 5 Notes

20. (page 88)
https://www.snopes.com/fact-check/barack-obama-2005-immigration-quote/

21. (page 88)
https://www.azquotes.com/author/11023-Barack_Obama/tag/immigration

22. (page 90)
Independent journalist Matt Taibbi says that Substack is "a relatively small company that's nonetheless one of the few oases of independent media and free speech left in America." See https://www.racket.news/p/meet-the-censored-me

— 6 —

A New World Order

6.1 Organizational Challenges (Top-down or bottom-up/middle-up): The Westphalian system or centralized world government? – by Nobuhiro Suzuki

The system in Japan seems like a cross between the Westphalian and the Centralized system. Harmony with other people is very important in Japan. Sometimes, it is more important than the freedom of individuals. It is good to cooperate with each other; but in some cases harmony can become strong peer pressure that may be linked to the uniformity of Japanese culture.

Centralized systems can easily work in Japan compared to Western countries. Most of the Japanese people follow the rules decided by the government, or other large organizations, without protest. Yes, there are some demonstrations in Japan when people have complaints. However, these are not aggressive.

You can read about examples of Japanese uniformity in Chapter 1. Most people who graduate from university (or high school) will start job hunting at the same time. Some rules – such as the timing of job hunting – are decided by the organization called "Nihon Keizai Dantai Rengou-

Kai (Keidanren)." Basically, big and famous companies tend to follow the rules, but some small companies don't.

In Japan, it is commonly agreed that young people should respect older people. Indeed, we need to use honorifics when we talk with older people. However, some old people think that young people must always follow what old people say. In addition, in many companies, most bosses are older and think that we must follow what they say. So, top-down decision making tends to be more general in Japan. In some cases, it is not easy for young people to give their opinions, and so innovative ideas are not generated.

However, uniformity (at least partially by peer pressure) can also positively affect societies. As mentioned above, the number of people infected by COVID-19 is lower in Japan compared to Western countries like the USA. Probably, one reason is that Japanese people follow the restrictions decided by the government. Based on the decision of the government, Japanese people stayed at home without complaining.

The case of Japan may show that a country's political system should not be too biased toward the Westphalian System or to centralized government. Each system has both advantages and disadvantages.

6.2 Centralization vs. Decentralization and Inclusive vs. Exclusive societies: What are the advantages and disadvantages? – by Nobuhiro Suzuki

The case of Japan shows that governance should not be too much biased toward centralization or decentralization. Centralized systems sometimes inhibit innovative work. In contrast, centralized systems may create greater harmony, and societies can solve large problems together.

One reason why Japanese people are harmonized and uniform may be that Japan is an isolated island country, and the diversity of races is very low. This situation creates an atmosphere of cooperation. Compared to western countries, Japan has much less motivation to accept immigrants from other countries.

Our history may make Japanese too shy to interact with people from other countries. I feel that Japanese who have lived in other countries for a long time are considered to be "different" from "standard" Japanese. Also, many Japanese still cannot speak English, irrespective of more than 10 years of English education. Thus, many Japanese people aren't used to interacting with people from other countries, or with Japanese people who are affected by foreign cultures.

If Japan accepts more immigrants from other countries, it may become much more inclusive. (I will not say that Japan is exclusive; rather, that Japanese are too shy to interact with people from other countries.)

Uniformity can become a big influence to solve large problems, when people work together. In this case, centralized government can be suitable. However, people who have similar personalities and characteristics may also have similar weaknesses.

Compared to the Japanese government, the U.S. government is more decentralized because many laws are different depending on the state.

Decentralized systems can be more flexible, and people can appeal at a more local level. Indeed, when I was in the USA, I felt a free atmosphere. However, the problem of decentralized systems became apparent around the election in 2020. Harmony between people was broken and many conflicts still continue.

We should not forget that both centralized and decentralized systems are a double-edged sword.

6.3 Differences in life and working styles: How are working styles different between US and Japan? – by Nobuhiro Suzuki

In Japan, many young people who just graduated from university or high school begin to work at the same time. They will experience many different types of work, such as sales, accounting, human resources, and so on, within the same company. I know some people who moved from the development department to the sales department. If you ask a Japanese person, "What is your job?" many Japanese tell you the name of the company they are working for. So, in Japan, people are required to serve in various types of jobs for companies, rather than one type of work that requires specific knowledge and skills.

As mentioned above, in Japan the interests of companies and organizations take precedence over the well-being of individuals. There are still some people who die because of overwork (this is known as Karoushi). Japanese have begun to change this situation, but the problem is still not completely solved. In addition, it is not easy sometimes to take a vacation, because of the work atmosphere of companies. Japanese think that it is not really good to take vacations when other people are working hard. It is likely that many Japanese do not use all of their paid vacation time.

I have not worked in companies in the USA, but I would like to describe what I think based on my experiences working in Japanese universities. In Japan, professors need to do many things, including administrative work, that is not directly related to research or teaching. This situation seems similar to the people working in companies. Probably, professors in Japanese universities perform more administrative and service work compared to those in U.S. universities. In some cases, university professors don't have enough time to do research or even to prepare for teaching because of their administrative duties (this is an anecdotal, generalized statement). In the USA, my boss was mainly doing research work because of his contract with the university. Other professors worked mainly on teaching. Duties in American universities are different depending on the professor. I imagine that, in the USA, it may be a similar situation for those who work in companies: The duties of people are determined according to their knowledge and skill sets.

In Japan, it is still not common to change companies. In many cases, a company may assume that an employee will work for a long duration (in general until retirement, approximately to the age of 60). Moreover, salaries will increase as employees get older. It is likely that such a company culture links to the type of job a person is working in, as they serve in many different roles for the company. However, the situation, especially for young people, has recently started to change. Some companies cannot guarantee salary increases because of the economic situation. Thus, some people work for a company only for a few years in order to gain work experience, then they try to change to another company that offers a better salary and more desirable working conditions.

6.4 The Westphalian System: Centralization vs. Decentralization – by Kenneth MacLean

The human race is now engaged in a war of ideas. In 2021 and 2022, this conflict emphasized debates around COVID-19: lockdowns, the nullification of individual freedoms in the name of public health, or the opening of economies so people can get on with their lives, and forced vaccinations / vaccine passports. Now it's about free speech. But the conversation around these topics merely features political mudslinging and make-wrong of those who have differing beliefs. The issue is much deeper than that, and literally involves how human societies in the future will be organized. The debate between centralization and decentralization is worldwide, and affects almost every human being on the planet.

In the West, the ideas of the nation state, sovereignty, and territorial integrity began in the 17th century with the signing of the Peace of Westphalia in 1648, which ended 80 years of war in Europe, and also involved a religious truce of sorts between the three main religions of that time: Roman Catholicism, Lutheranism (based on the doctrines of Martin Luther, which were essentially objections to the perceived corruption in the Catholic Church), and Calvinism. The Peace of Westphalia was the beginning of the modern era of nation states with distinct and protected cultural, religious, and/or political identities. The concepts of territorial integrity and national sovereignty were born out of these negotiations almost 400 years ago. These ideas allowed for the establishment of the United Nations in 1945, just after World War II.

The 20th century saw the establishment of communist and fascist states, and a serious challenge to the Westphalian system across the globe. Of course there have always been totalitarian states throughout human history, but as the population of earth rose from 2 billion in 1927 to 7 billion in 2011, centralization, authoritarianism, and centrally planned economies began to conflict with notions of individual rights, and societies such as constitutional republics that protect individual freedoms.

Those in favor of centralization argue that planned economies are vastly more efficient at moving goods and services, and are better able to utilize the talents of individuals in society for the common good. Those in favor of decentralization decry the squelching of human rights and individual freedoms, and argue that centralized societies inevitably become totalitarian, inhibit creativity, and are ruled by a privileged elite who use inflexible ideology to make people follow "the party line." Those in favor of centralization counter that the inevitable evolution of free societies leads also to the establishment of wealthy elites who establish a modern-day privileged class of oligarchs who lord it over the people.

In the United States there is a lot of confusion about the political system we have. If you asked most citizens about this, they would say that the US is a democracy. On a very basic level, this is true. But the US is actually a representative federal constitutional republic. Our Constitution and Bill of Rights spell out explicitly what the government can and cannot do. The Bill of Rights codifies individual rights for each citizen, and religious rights. According to the U.S. constitution, these rights come directly from God, and not the State. The power of the central government is limited by the Constitution, and all powers not specifically granted to the central government are reserved to the states.

Here is what the 10th Amendment to the Constitution says:

"The powers not delegated to the United States by the Constitution, nor prohibited by it to the States, are reserved to the States respectively, or to the people."

FindLaw says:

> Passed by Congress in 1789 and ratified in 1791, the Tenth Amendment is the last in the group of Constitutional Amendments known as the Bill of Rights. Unlike several of the other early amendments, it is quite brief – only one sentence. But that one sentence grants state governments all powers not specifically delegated to the federal government by the Constitution. However, as broad a grant as this seems, interpretation by the Supreme Court has placed some limits on state power.
>
> **Frequently Asked Questions**
>
> What is meant by "reserved powers?"
>
> "Reserved powers" refers to powers that are not specifically

granted to the federal government by the Constitution. The Tenth Amendment gives these powers to the states.

What is an example of a reserved power?

Reserved powers include running elections, creating marriage laws, and regulating schools.

Why are reserved powers important?

Reserving powers for state governments helps maintain a balance of power between the states and the federal government. They also allow states the freedom to try out different ideas and programs, which is why states are sometimes called "laboratories of democracy."[23]

Furthermore, in *Fry v. United States, 421 U.S. 542, 547 n.7* (1975), the 10th Amendment expressly declares the constitutional policy that Congress may not exercise power in a fashion that impairs the States' integrity or their ability to function effectively in a federal system.[24]

In the United States, the states are the laboratories of democracy. That's the meaning of "United States." The Constitution and the Bill of Rights were written precisely to limit the power of centralization by the British crown, or any dictator or group of totalitarians, such as modern-day fascists, communists, medical and technical bureaucracies, and what is called the national security state.

The states run elections and have always run elections, not the federal government in DC. The power to examine elections and ballots can be performed by the duly elected legislatures of each state.

In the United States, there is good reason to limit the power of the central government, simply because of the diversity of races and cultures here. In a more homogeneous society like Japan, common bonds of culture and history create greater harmony and collective agreement.

In a democracy, the majority can trample on the rights of minorities.

The Electoral College, for example, was designed to protect the rights of less populated states from the rule of big states. Those who favor abolition of the Electoral College, or packing the Supreme Court (or even the abolishment of the Senate) have, most likely, not studied the U.S. Constitution and the checks and balances it creates to keep a stable political system. The 2020 riots in dozens of American cities is a taste of what can happen when mob rule takes over. Totalitarian societies are always centralized, and are always based on intolerance for other points of view.

Here in the US there is now a debate between a populist movement that favors a smaller government and a larger private sector, and those who favor the centralized model of a huge central government that plans the lives of all citizens. Under the guise of "COVID relief bills" (The American Recovery Act) and "inflation reduction" (The so-called Inflation Reduction Act), and other supplemental spending, the central government in Washington DC – using the Federal Reserve, the nation's central bank – is literally printing trillions of unfunded dollars.

Where this will lead is anyone's guess, but one thing is certain: money is not wealth. As long as the amount of currency and credit in circulation balances the goods and services produced by the economy, the currency is stable, inflation is low, and the economy has the opportunity to run well. Merely printing money without a concomitant increase in the production of goods and services must lead inevitably to inflation and the debasing of the currency, which adversely affects the poor, those least able to withstand the onslaught of inflation. Inflating the currency has been tried (and it has failed) throughout history, from the Roman Empire to the U.S. colonies, who attempted to print scrip to fund the Revolutionary War against the British crown. This currency was just pieces of paper backed by nothing valuable.

A centralized economy would be able to print massive amounts of money, whereas a decentralized economy with a smaller central government and a large private sector would never be able to get away with it.

In short, centralized governments can never plan for the billions of decisions made every day by citizens. Centralized planning inevitably results in prohibition on thought, speech, and action to suit the demands of those in power. This is why centralized, totalitarian societies have always failed.

In conclusion, human societies thrive when they are supported by the rule of law, and by the guarantee of liberty and freedom of thought and expression, which leads to creativity and powerful economic opportunities. Although some centralization is necessary for good planning and rational public policy, too much centralization will lead to a sterile and stagnant society ruled by a privileged few.

Chapter 6 Notes

23. (page 99)

FindLaw staff, "The Tenth Amendment: Reserving Power for the States," https://constitution.findlaw.com/amendment10.html

24. (page 99)

Id.

—7—

What Should be the Goals of the World Community?

by Nobuhiro Suzuki

This chapter will consider the traditional cultures and customs that have been specifically established in our own countries.

I write from the perspective of a biologist. Biological systems may provide useful information about how to unite with others. In a cell of any organism, numerous genes, proteins, and compounds are working together to make the entire cell healthy. For multicellular organisms, such complex systems maintain the homeostasis of the entire body. In addition, organisms are capable of adapting to a fluctuating environment by modulating complex systems in cells. Furthermore, interactions between different organisms – from microorganisms to mammal – are necessary to maintain environmental conditions. Therefore, in biological systems, many different things nicely communicate with each other to make their own world comfortable. Human beings can learn a lot from nature.

Let's proceed with that idea in mind.

Each country in the world has its own traditional culture and customs. However, it is getting harder to maintain some of these traditions, because the world situation is always changing. We are moving toward "globalization" with the internet, and it has become much easier to know the cultures and customs of other countries. In some cases, these foreign cultures and customs look excellent, and dramatically affect how people think. Thus, many people, especially the young generations, want change to make their lives more fulfilling. Several local and traditional cultures and customs may not be suitable for the current situation, and they negatively affect people's lives. Consequently, these cultures and customs will change, or even disappear. However, there are still many people who don't want to change their cultural traditions. Conflicts in the world seem to be "new" vs "traditional." Perhaps it is time to consider different opinions.

Of course, it is better for people to change traditional customs and accept the new ways, if such changes make everyone happy. However, can there be cultural changes that make all people happy? We cannot ignore the fact that some traditions are still important and should not be changed. It is necessary for us to consider which traditions we should change and which should not be changed. Cultural traditions were established because they were necessary for people. Therefore, we should learn how and why our traditions were established in history, and consider how these traditions affect our current lives. Some traditions may still be very important for us, but others are not and could even negatively affect our lives.

We should not ignore the fact that traditional cultures and customs have been established in each country in unique ways. Traditional customs were established to make people's lives comfortable and were dependent on the climate, natural environment, and characteristics of each country. Therefore, traditions that have been established in one country may not be suitable for other countries. In addition, it is also important to be flexible. Traditions that are not suitable for the current situation may be important in the future. Conversely, currently important customs may be viewed as garbage in future generations! Also, the world climate is changing and it may affect our lifestyles.

In Japan, for example, the cultural tradition is that the oldest son of a family should take over the house, properties, family grave, and job from his father, and that he has a responsibility to keep them. Another important traditional cultural norm in Japan is to keep the family tree. This has been common to both rural and urban areas. Recently, however, these traditions have been changing. It is getting harder and harder for the oldest son to take over a house and properties from his father if the family lives in a rural area, because the economy of many rural areas in Japan is getting worse, and it is very hard (or almost impossible) to hold a job handed down from the father. If the oldest son does not take over his father's job, it is very hard to find a new job in rural areas. So, many young people move to urban areas to get a job and do not take over the house, properties, and family grave. Even in urban areas, young people are starting to make their own decisions about their lives and are no longer obsessed with keeping the family tree.

Some readers might know young people who don't like learning history, and wonder why we need to learn it. I would like to suggest that learning history is important to prevent conflicts, because we can understand the background of specific cultures and customs in different countries. This understanding allows us to know how and why we are different, and may be a catalyst to stop conflicts. In addition, we learn a lot about past wars from the history books. It is important to learn more deeply how and why these wars started, and obtain hints to prevent future conflicts. Cultural and historical knowledge about other countries is important to make a good world community.

What Should be the Goals of the World Community?

by Kenneth MacLean

In response to this question I have chosen to play Devil's Advocate. A world community is a nice idea, but the consciousness of the human race is not yet ready for it. To understand this, watch a United Nations telecast!

A true world community is only possible when human beings put away their childish and petty hatreds, their selfishness, and their greed. When will that occur? I don't know – perhaps in some distant future.

Instead of thinking about a world community, let us think in terms of diversity. By diversity I don't mean a conception based merely on gender and race, which only recognizes physical characteristics. As Martin Luther King famously said, "I have a dream that my four little children will one day live in a nation where they will not be judged by the color of their skin but by *the content of their character.*" [italics mine]

Dr. King's brilliant formulation for the worth of a human being relies not on materialist concepts like race or gender. It is a formulation based on consciousness, the quality of one's character. Here we come to the heart of the matter.

A materialist conception of consciousness says that self-awareness comes from neurons firing in the brain, and that when your body dies, you're dead. The greedy, the selfish, the power-mad, all believe this wholeheartedly. A more positive view of consciousness says that a human being has a divine component that is inherently linked to human biology. That divine component is the creative and cooperative power in all of us.

A world community has never really been able to come to fruition because humanity has embraced a false definition of consciousness: one that says human nature is inherently greedy and selfish. This conception follows directly from the materialist conception of consciousness, which is rooted in a "service to self" conception. A true world community would be oriented on a "service to others" formulation.

A more realistic world community would be concerned with diversity. Not the diversity of race and gender, but the diversity of opinion. This diversity would celebrate culture and be truly inclusive, welcoming all points of view, and thus create an information-rich, creative community. It may be composed of nation-states, or cultural blocs that transcend national boundaries. This conception is much different from patriotism or nationalism, which has been the match that has lit numerous wars.

The English word that best describes a true world community is acceptance.

Acceptance precludes bickering, argumentation, hatred, and violence because someone has a different opinion.

Acceptance requires a very high level of consciousness. The human race is a long way from that.

If it is not possible, now, to create a true world community, what is a realistic goal?

1) Eliminate world hunger. This is #2 on the UN's Sustainable Goals list.

The planet can produce an abundance of food. Our inefficient supply chains and distribution systems are the problem. These problems exist because of greed, selfishness, and excessive national and corporate competition.

There is only one item on this list. That's because solving world hunger will largely solve the rest of humanity's problems. Moreover, ending world hunger is not a political issue. It does, however, strike at the heart of selfishness, greed, and irrational national and corporate competition for resources. The UN's sustainable goals for the planet encompass

17 items! Each of them, individually, is an almost impossible goal.

Rather than dividing our attention, let's focus our world community objectives on eliminating world hunger. As the British say, "That's enough to be going on with."

Afterword

How can misunderstanding be prevented? It is important to accept different ideas and cultures. The ideas and cultures of each country have been long established historically. And so we shouldn't deny each other's way of thinking, and culture, for the sake of immediate profit.

It is a simple thing to write this, but much harder to accept cultural differences and norms. This is an important issue in all world communications.

We should not forget that our current behavior may affect our culture. We began to write this book in 2020; but now, in 2023, the world has changed dramatically. Such fast changes may have already established new ideas and cultural norms for young people and for our descendants in the future. For the peaceful future of the world, we should now direct our focus to harmony, not conflict.

— Nobuhiro Suzuki, April 2023

Nobu beautifully summarizes the intent of this book in his conclusion: Our communications establish new cultural norms and affect the intellectual and cultural development of the upcoming generation. What we write and say on social media therefore assumes immense importance.

The root cause of conflict and war is misunderstanding, which requires hatred, anger, and misinformation. Understanding is based on sharing and openness and transparency, qualities which are inherent to every human being. It begins with acceptance, or at least tolerance, of opposing points of view. Acceptance and understanding is so much easier and benefits everyone!

I hope that our little book will spur others to write and speak and affirm the things that bind us together, and our common humanity, to the benefit of everyone in the world. In order to do that we must maintain a free flow of ideas and a diversity of opinion, which is the fountainhead for new ideas and new approaches that can change the world.

— *Kenneth MacLean, April 2023*

About the Authors

Nobuhiro Suzuki

Nobuhiro obtained his M.Sc degree at Kagawa University in Japan in 2003, and his PhD from the University of Nevada, Reno, in 2009.

Nobu then worked as a post-doctoral fellow at the University of Nevada, Reno, from 2009–2010 and at the University of North Texas from 2010–2014.

He then became an Assistant Professor at Sophia University, in Tokyo, Japan beginning in 2014, and was promoted to Associate Professor in 2019.

Nobu's expertise is in plant physiology and plant molecular biology, focusing on the responses of plants to environmental stresses.

Kenneth MacLean

Ken has a B.A. in Political science and a B.S. in Computer Science. He is the author of 10 books and numerous blog articles.

Ken has been studying science and metaphysics for decades, in an attempt to explain the untimely death of his mother from leukemia at the age of 28. Ken is a freelance writer and researcher, and an editor. He is interested in geometry and has written a textbook describing important 3 dimensional solids called polyhedra.

Ken is an accomplished editor with experience in creative writing, academic witting, and technical manuals.

Ken has not lived in an ivory tower. For 25 years he owned a contracting business in which he met people from all walks of life. From these experiences Ken learned how to relate to the poor and the rich, the uneducated and university professors, and people from different cultures and religions. Ken has learned that the common denominator of all human beings is a divine presence that transcends cultural and religious backgrounds. This understanding is reflected in all of his work.

Ken's favorite quote is from John Payne: "True love is empowering people to see their greater potential."

Ken has been happily married for 44 years to Jennifer, and lives in Ann Arbor, Michigan with their two cats.

Ken's books can be found on his website at kj-maclean.com/Products/MainProductPage.php, and on Amazon.com under the names "Kenneth MacLean," Kenneth J. MacLean," and "Kenneth J.M. MacLean."

Index

www.ingramcontent.com/pod-product-compliance
Lightning Source LLC
LaVergne TN
LVHW010111170826
845678LV00012B/2357

* 9 7 8 1 6 1 5 9 9 8 6 3 0 *